The Japanese Abacus

NOTE

The Publisher is pleased to announce, for the benefit of readers who have had difficulty in obtaining abacuses, that Japanese-made instruments of fine quality in various sizes are now available in the United States as listed below:

Small	(13 rods)
Medium	(15 rods)
Large	(23 rods)

Please inquire from Charles E. Tuttle Company, Rutland, Vermont. Mail orders promptly filled.

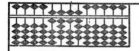

The
JAPANESE ABACUS
Its Use and Theory

BY

TAKASHI KOJIMA

CHARLES E. TUTTLE COMPANY
RUTAND VERMONT   TOKYO JAPAN

Published by the Charles E. Tuttle Company, Inc.
of Rutland, Vermont & Tokyo, Japan

Editorial offices:
Suido 1-chome, 2-6, Bunkyo-ku
Tokyo, Japan

Library of Congress Catalog Card No. 55-3550

International Standard Book No. 0-8048-0278-5

First edition, April 1954
Thirty-fourth printing, 1991

Printed in Japan

CONTENTS

FOREWORD

It gives me great pleasure that this book in English on the abacus is ready for publication. Japanese abacus operators have long cherished the desire, here finally realised, of introducing the Japanese abacus to other countries in view of the remarkable advances and developments which have been made in the instrument and its use during the past quarter of a century.

The Japanese abacus, simple and primitive looking though it be, can be operated with greater speed and efficiency than even the electric calculating machine—a fact proven in numerous tests and well documented by Mr. Kojima in his first chapter. This is particulary so in addition and subtraction, where the abacus can handle figures of any number of digits twice as fast as the electric machine. To explain the instrument's incredible speed and mystifying efficiency it is essential not only to introduce the newest improved methods of operation but also to elucidate the most advanced theories of rational bases and of bead manipulation.

In writing this practical book Mr. Kojima has kept these two requirements well in mind. The Abacus Research Institute of the Japan Chamber of Commerce and Industry has been most pleased to cooperate with him by making available its research data and correcting his manuscript in the light of all the latest information.

YOEMON YAMAZAKI

Vice-Chairman, Abacus Research Institute
Professor of Economics, Nihon University
Vice-President, All-Japan Federation of Abacus Operators

AUTHOR'S FOREWORD

This book has been written as a guide for those who, though interested in knowing more about the use and theory of the Japanese abacus, have until now been unable to find any full explanation in the English language. Chapter I presents the most important facts about the speed and efficiency of abacus calculation, with special reference to a comparison of the abacus and the electric calculating machine. Chapter II gives a brief survey of the history and development of the abacus, and Chapter III introduces the basic principles of abacus calculation.

The next three chapters explain in detail, with numerous examples, how the four processes of arithmetic are worked out on the abacus. Particular attention should be given to Chapter IV, on addition and subtraction, as it embodies the essential rules of bead manipulation. Many notes have been included to give a theoretical and scientific explanation of the rules and fundamental principles as such knowledge is not only of interest but will prove of great aid in the actual operation of the instrument. The book concludes with short chapters on decimals and mental calculation, and a selection of exercises.

Among many who kindly gave me information and suggestions, I am particularly grateful to Mr. Yoemon Yamazaki, who kindly wrote the foreword and provided me with many valuable suggestions and a large part of the information in Chapter I. He is the Vice-Chairman of the Abacus Research Institute and Advisor to the Central Committee of the Federation of Abacus Workers (hereafter referred to simply as the Abacus Committee), both organizations being under the sponsorship of the Japan

Chamber of Commerce and Industry.

I also wish to express my special gratitude to Mr. Shinji Ishikawa, President of the Japan Association of Abacus Calculation, who spared himself no trouble in reading the whole of the manuscript and furnishing much important up-to-date information.

I also extend my grateful acknowledgements to Mr. Zenji Arai, Chairman of the Abacus Research Committee of the Japan Federation of Abacus Education, and Mr. Miyokichi Ban, of the above-mentioned Abacus Committee. They kindly read the whole of the manuscript and provided me with many necessary and valuable suggestions.

My grateful acknowledgements are also due to Mr. Takeo Uno on the Abacus Committee and Mr. Tadao Yamamoto, who conducts his own abacus school. They kindly read the manuscript in parts and gave me valuable suggestions.

I also wish to thank Mr. Kiyoshi Matsuzaki, of the Savings Bureau of the Ministry of Postal Administration, who kindly furnished the table on page 13.

Finally I must express my sincere thanks for many invaluable suggestions on English style from Mr. C. G. Wells, Chief Writer for the Far East Network; Mr. Harold Gosling, of the British Commonwealth Public Relations; Mr. Richard D. Lane, formerly of the Far East Network; and above all from Mr. Meredith Weatherby, of the Charles E. Tuttle Company, without whose painstaking efforts this book could not have become what it is now.

T. K.

I. ABACUS VERSUS ELECTRIC CALCULATOR

The abacus, or *soroban* as it is called in Japan, is one of the first objects that strongly attract the attention of the foreigner in Japan. When he buys a few trifling articles at some store, he soon notices that the tradesman does not perplex himself with mental arithmetic, but instead seizes his *soroban*, prepares it by a tilt and a rattling sweep of his hand, and after a deft manipulation of rapid clicks, reads off the price. It is true that the Japanese tradesman often uses his board and beads even when the problem is simple enough to be done in one's head, but this is only because the use of the abacus has become a habit with him. If he tried, he could no doubt easily add 37 and 48 in his head. But such is the force of habit that he does not try to recognize the simplicity of any problem; instead, following the line of least resistance, he adjusts his *soroban* for manipulation, and begins clicking the beads, thus escaping any need of mental effort.

Doubtlessly the Westerner, with his belief in the powers of mental arithmetic and the modern calculating machine, often mistrusts the efficiency of such a primitive looking instrument. However, his mistrust of the *soroban* is likely to be transformed into admiration when he gains some knowledge concerning it. For the *soroban*, which can perform in a fraction of time a difficult arithmetic calculation that the Westerner could do laboriously only by means of pencil and paper, possesses distinct advantages over mental and written arithmetic. In a competition in arithmetic problems, an ordinary Japanese tradesman with his *soroban* would easily outstrip a rapid and accurate Western accountant even with his adding machine.

An exciting contest between the Japanese abacus and the electric calculating machine was held in Tokyo on November 12, 1946, under the sponsorship of the U. S. Army newspaper, the *Stars and Stripes*. In reporting the contest, the *Stars and Stripes* remarked : " The machine age took a step backward yesterday at the Ernie Pyle Theater as the abacus, centuries old, dealt defeat to the most up-to-date electric machine now being used by the United States Government . . . The abacus victory was decisive."

The *Nippon Times* reported the contest as follows : " Civilization, on the threshold of the atomic age, tottered Monday afternoon as the 2,000-year-old abacus beat the electric calculating machine in adding, subtracting, dividing and a problem including all three with multiplication thrown in, according to UP. Only in multiplication alone did the machine triumph. . . ."

The American representative of the calculating machine was Pvt. Thomas Nathan Wood of the 240th Finance Disbursing Section of General MacArthur's headquarters, who had been selected in an arithmetic contest as the most expert operator of the electric calculator in Japan. The Japanese representative was Mr. Kiyoshi Matsuzaki, a champion operator of the abacus in the Savings Bureau of the Ministry of Postal Administration.

As may be seen from the results tabulated on the following page, the abacus scored a total of 4 points as against 1 point for the electric calculator. Such results should convince even the most skeptical that, at least so far as addition and subtraction are concerned, the abacus possesses an indisputable advantage over the calculating machine. Its advantages in the fields of multiplication and division, however, were not so decisively demonstrated:

RESULTS OF CONTEST

MATSUZAKI (Abacus) vs. WOOD (Electric Calculator)

Type of Problem	Name	1st Heat	2nd Heat	3rd Heat	Score
Addition: 50 numbers each consisting of from 3 to 6 digits	Matsuzaki	1m. 14.8s. Victor	1m. 16s. Victor		1
	Wood	2m. 0.2s. Defeated	1m. 53s. Defeated		
Subtraction: 5 problems, with minuends and subtrahends of from 6 to 8 digits each	Matsuzaki	1m. 0.4s. All correct Victor	1m. 0.8s. 4 correct No decision	1m. All correct Victor	1
	Wood	1m. 30s. All correct Defeated	1m. 36s. 4 correct No decision	1m. 22s. 4 correct Defeated	
Multiplication: 5 problems, each containing 5 to 12 digits in multiplier and multiplicand	Matsuzaki	1m. 44.6s. 4 correct Defeated	1m. 19s. All correct Victor	2m. 14.4s. 3 correct Defeated	
	Wood	2m. 22s. 4 correct Victor	1m. 20s. All correct Defeated	1m. 53.6s. 4 correct Victor	1
Division: 5 problems, each containing 5 to 12 digits in divisor and dividend	Matsuzaki	1m. 36.6s. All correct Victor	1m. 23.4s. 4 correct Defeated	1m. 21s. All correct Victor	1
	Wood	1m. 48s. All correct Defeated	1m. 19s. All correct Victor	1m. 26.6s. 4 correct Defeated	
Composite problem: 1 problem in addition of 30 6-digit numbers; 3 problems in subtraction, each with two 6-digit numbers; 3 problems in multiplication, each with two figures containing a total of 5 to 12 digits; 3 problems in division, each with two figures containing a total of 5 to 12 digits	Matsuzaki	1m. 21s. All correct Victor			1
	Wood	1m. 26.6s. 4 correct Defeated			
Total Score	Matsuzaki				4
	Wood				1

For reliable information on the comparative merits of the abacus and the calculating machine, we can do nothing better then turn to the Abacus Committee of the Japan Chamber of Commerce and Industry, which has made minute investigations concerning the potentialities of the Japanese abacus. The Committee has acted as judge of the semi-annual examination for abacus operators' licenses since the examinations were initiated in 1931, such licenses being divided into three classes, according to the manipulators' efficiency.

The Committee says: "In a contest in addition and subtraction, a first-grade abacus operator can easily defeat the best operator of an electric machine, solving problems twice as fast as the latter, no matter how many digits the numbers contain. If the numbers do not contain over six digits, the abacus manipulator can halve the time of the operation by relying in part upon mental calculation (a system peculiar to the abacus, to be described hereafter). In multiplication and division the first-grade abacus operator can maintain some margin of advantage over the electric calculator so long as the problem does not contain more than a total of about ten digits in multiplicand and multiplier or in divisor and quotient. The abacus and the electric machine are on a par in a problem which contains a total of ten to twelve digits. With each additional digit in a problem, the advantage of the electric calculating machine increases."

A similar view is held by Mr. Kiyoshi Matsuzaki, who made the following remark concerning the contest described in preceding pages: "In addition and subtraction even the third-grade abacus worker can hold his own against the electric calculating machine. In multiplication and division the first-grade abacus worker may have a good chance to win over the calculating machine, provided the problem does not have more than a total of ten digits in multiplicand and multiplier or in divisor and quotient. I felt nervous at the contest and made more mistakes than I might have done otherwise. My opponent may have felt the same, though. A good first-grade abacus worker ought to be able to make a better showing when he is at ease."

As examples of the proficiency required of the abacus operator, it will be of interest to cite a few problems used in the examination for abacus operators' licences.

A. ADDITION AND SUBTRACTION

No.	1	2	3	4	5
1	¥ 6,395,082.74	¥40,693,718.52	¥ 160,384.72	¥ 730.49	¥ 352,719.48
2	269.31	52,687.09	83,479,051.26	6,089,547.31	84,936.20
3	541,793.60	7,180,592.43	− 21,479.50	463,195.28	92,460,385.71
4	82,706,314.95	1,745.38	9,058,627.13	97,820.56	−718,024.36
5	72,940.18	63,847,529.10	−3,780.29	3,985,271.04	45,178.62
6	3,014,725.86	26,073.94	27,915.64	10,476,825.93	8,327,605.94
7	98,156.02	309,861.75	40,715,368.92	54,613.78	−19,062.53
8	15,726,408.39	8,714,905.26	86,223.41	218,769.45	−4,083,237.61
9	970,285.13	346.17	−504,189.76	3,428.01	25,963,180.47
10	45,963.78	295,130.86	− 6,037,512.89	82,605,917.34	70,941.28
11	6,831,750.24	94,038,726.51	924.35	61,853.20	−6,798.05
12	64,371.59	69,052.74	763,815.04	250,376.19	−50,824,361.79
13	249,168.07	150,938.42	− 20,849,136.57	3,576,904.82	953.16
14	70,593,826.41	43,281.65	4,102,653.98	49,021.67	3,107,425.89
15	4,352.80	7,916,403.28	95,467.83	57,316,482.90	639,507.14
計					

B. MULTIPLICATION

No. 1	$759.843 \times 57.941 =$
2	$302.162 \times 83.602 =$
3	$967.408 \times 70.589 =$
4	$20.359 \times 628.134 =$
5	$84.2697 \times 9.4076 =$
6	$135.941 \times 46.295 =$
7	$0.4271805 \times 0.2513 =$
8	$669.378 \times 0.31908 =$
9	$0.914053 \times 68.037 =$
10	$587.216 \times 17.452 =$

C. DIVISION

No. 1	$4,768,788,098 \div 14,593 =$
2	$971,337,349 \div 51.682 =$
3	$47,408,509,168 \div 49.201 =$
4	$0.3481095257 \div 0.06457 =$
5	$66,014,150,202 \div 92,378 =$
6	$3,657.6146092 \div 80,914 =$
7	$166.4719833 \div 0.6702 =$
8	$0.4537275087 \div 7.38609 =$
9	$328,399.09042 \div 35.746 =$
10	$24,484,596,290 \div 28.135 =$

D.   MENTAL CALCULATION

No.	1	2	3	4	5
1	¥ 74.63	¥ 3.46	¥ 52.31	¥ 8.09	¥ 90.47
2	2.98	97.98	30.64	2.41	3.51
3	50.41	6.05	−9.28	56.37	−76.29
4	83.72	2.13	14.75	1.52	−1.83
5	1.35	50.79	8.39	70.86	54.02
6	6.84	8.21	−45.05	3.94	8.35
7	95.01	19.64	6.17	96.70	29.14
8	3.27	78.30	−2.83	6.28	−6.50
9	65.10	4.56	7.14	37.19	47.26
10	4.92	82.07	91.26	48.05	1.83
計					

To receive a first-grade license an applicant must be able to work problems similar to the foregoing with 80 per cent accuracy within a time limit of five minutes each for the first three groups—A, B and C—and one minute for the fourth.

The problem in mental calculation requires a few words of explanation as the method of solving it depends directly upon a knowledge of the use of the abacus, and being an integral part of abacus technique, it is entirely different from any Western method of calculation. This abacus method of mental arithmetic is described in some detail in Chapter VIII. Suffice is to say here that the method consists in mentally visualizing an abacus and working the problem out by standard methods on the imaginary instrument. The process is easier than it sounds and accounts for the incredible and almost mystifying peaks of efficiency attained by masters of abacus operation.

To cite but one example of proficiency in this type of mental arithmetic, on May 28, 1952, during the Sixth All-Japan Abacus Contest, held in Tokyo, a master abacus operator, Mr. Yoshio Kojima, gave a demonstration of his skill in mental arithmetic.

In one minute and 18.4 seconds he gave correct answer to 50 division problems, each of which contained five to seven digits in its dividend and divisor. Next, in a twinkling of 13.6 seconds he added 10 numbers of ten digits each. Thus he set two remarkable records—and all with no aid other than the mentally visualized abacus! This means that he could have added mentally the fifteen numbers given in one of the columns

A. ADDITION AND SUBTRACTION

1	¥ 71,896	¥ 93,502	¥ 130,745	¥ 60,374	¥ 9,180
2	306,425	8,164	59,280	875,126	25,634
3	839	802,635	4,968	23,601	418,275
4	50,178	378	102	7,284	54,361
5	2,941	25,910	701,539	932	7,903
6	567,308	−8,756	48,075	−506,849	86,215
7	762	650,481	6,714	−39,256	903,587
8	82,037	362	429	1,023	643
9	3,694	71,049	602,893	485	71,852
10	470,589	2,913	27,564	187,683	408
11	24,310	134,795	4,931	−96,178	640,729
12	165	−19,247	93,270	−4,517	210
13	5,742	−804	315,687	−760	92,674
14	904,213	−65,798	90,312	248,951	5,096
15	68,951	746,083	856	19,074	837,921
計					

B. MULTIPLICATION

No.	
1	$6,742 \times 358 =$
2	$2,681 \times 609 =$
3	$5,093 \times 176 =$
4	$0.825 \times 94.12 =$
5	$3,310 \times 803 =$
6	$9,478 \times 0.645 =$
7	$76,506 \times 5.2 =$
8	193.4×4.18
9	$0.4052 \times 0.267 =$
10	$9,718 \times 703 =$

C. DIVISION

No.	
1	$435,633 \div 921 =$
2	$315,56 \div 805 =$
3	$18.998 \div 236 =$
4	$63.162 \div 0.087 =$
5	$223.792 \div 394 =$
6	$400.026 \div 418 =$
7	$180,096 \div 64$
8	$0.105118 \div 0.753 =$
9	$104,249 \div 1.709 =$
10	$0.21918 \div 5.62 =$

of Problem A, page 15, in one-fourth of the given time limit of one minute, and in one-eighth of the time required by the best operator of an electric calculating machine.

To receive a third-grade license an applicant must be able to work problems similar to those on page 17 with 70 per cent accuracy within a time limit of five minutes for each group.

The primary advantage of the abacus is its incredible speed resulting from the mechanization or simplification of calculation, by means of which the answer to a given problem forms itself naturally or mechanically on the board, thus reducing mental labor to a minimum. The theoretical explanation of this mechanization of calculation is given in Chapter IV (see Note 3 to Example 9, Note 3 to Example 10, and Notes 3, 4 and 5 to Example 20).

Another big advantage of the abacus is its extremely moderate price, ranging generally between 25¢ and $2.50 or $3.50 to quote prices in U.S. dollar equivalents. How many times more does the ordinary calculating machine cost, to say nothing of the gleaming electric machines which abound in Western business houses?

Among many other merits of the abacus one should not overlook its handy construction, its portability, and the ease of its operational methods, which are nothing more than simplifications of the four processes of arithmetic.

The most peculiar advantage of the abacus is that a problem in addition and subtraction is worked out from left to right instead of from right to left as is the case with written arithmetic, and thus harmonizes perfectly with the normal way of reading and writing numbers. In this way a number can be added or subtracted while it is being given. For example, if the first number in the problem is 753, the operator can enter 7 on the abacus the instant he hears or sees " seven hundred," and then proceed on next to the 5 and finally the 3, whereas in written calculation he would usually have to wait until all figures were given and then start calculating backward from the 3 of 753.

The one admitted disadvantage of the abacus is that the instrument produces only a final result without preserving any record of intermediate steps. If any error is made, the whole calculation must be carried through again from beginning to end. But this seeming disadvantage is more than offset by the rapidity and accuracy which the abacus makes possible. And it is the result that counts.

The chief factor which discredits the abacus in Western eyes is the length of time and practice required to become a skilled operator. Certainly the abacus requires much more practice than the calculating machine. But this apparent disadvantage is not so great an obstacle as it is generally thought to be. Some experience and practice with this simple but highly scientific instrument will convince the reader that this Western idea is largely a prejudice. A few weeks of practice for an hour each day with proper procedures will give anyone sufficient skill to turn to the abacus instead of pencil and paper for arithmetical computation.

According to the Abacus Committee, average students, who begin their practice while in their teens, should be able to pass the examination for third-grade licenses after half a year of daily practice of one hour, and bright students or students with a mathematical bent after only three months. Generally speaking, another half year of practice will enable a third-grade abacus operator to obtain a second-grade license ; and one more full year should make him a first-grade operator. As is generally the case with any other art or accomplishment, it is best to start practising under right guidance when young. Those who take up their study of the abacus after they are out of their teens are never able to pass the first-grade examination, but it is definitely possible for them to attain to the third rank, and occasionally even to the second.

Recent years have shown the abacus to enjoy an amazing increase in popularity in Japan. In 1965 nearly one million applicants took the examinations, about a fourth of whom passed (roughly 5,000 out of 55,000 received first-grade licenses; 25,000 out of 280,000, second-grade; and 230,000 out of 750,000, third-grade). In the same year about half a million took the exam held by the National Federation of Abacus Operators, a private association independent of the All-Japan Federation of Abacus Operation which is affiliated with the Japan Chamber of Commerce and Industry. Additionally, another half a million took the exam held by the National Association of Vocation High School Principals.

The abacus has even found its way into the curriculum of all grade schools as one of the elements of arithmetic, and there are now numerous abacus schools to meet the needs of those preparing to go into business. In short, the abacus has become such a popular favorite that it is to be found in practically every household.

How are we to account for the sudden spurt in the popularity of the old-fashioned abacus, here in the middle of the mechanized twentieth century? Undoubtedly the principal explanation lies in the fact that its operational methods have recently been markedly simplified and improved. As will be explained in Chapter VI, the old method of division required the memorization of a difficult division table, and was the chief factor which alienated the average, non-commercial Japanese from the abacus. Once this difficulty was overcome by the introduction of the newer method of division—so much simpler and, in a sense, so much more accurate that it marked a milestone in the improvement of abacus technique—the instrument rapidly attained the universal popularity which it now enjoys.

But how account for the almost exclusive use of the abacus in offices and firms which could well afford electric calculating machines ? Let statistics give the answer. According to figures compiled by the Abacus Committe, in the conduct of an average business the four types of arithmetical calculation occur in about the following proportions : addition seventy percent, subtraction five percent, multiplication twenty percent, and division five percent As previously mentioned, the abacus can add and subtract faster than the electric calculating machine. As for problems in multiplication and division, those which contain more than a total of ten digits in their mutiplicand and multiplier or in their divisor and quotient are exceptional. This means that a good operator can work out most mutiplication and division problems as fast as or even faster on an abacus than on an electric calculation machine, to say nothing of the much slower non-electric machine. So even today when Japanese businesses are fitted with a variety of electronic computers, it is not surprising that the abacus retains its popularity with the tiny store as well as the giant corporation. To give figures, in Japanese businesses 85 per cent of all calculation is done on the abacus while most of the remainder is done on machines with a small percentage on calculating table, slide rules, or written or mental arithmetic.

At the present time various experiments are being undertaken to improve still further the operational technique of the abacus. But this little handbook will introduce only the best of the established methods and verified theories, essential for learning to operate the abacus with good understanding and rapidity. Once the basic rules have been mastered, the secret of acquiring skill in abacus operation lies in constant daily practice.

Problems involving the extraction of roots can also be solved on the abacus with great rapidity. But the extraction of roots, which is rarely used in everyday and business calculation, is outside the scope of this book.

The abacus can be also a great aid in the instruction of arithmetic in grade school. For about 50% of all problems in elementary school textbooks of arithmetic are calculation problems, and the other 50% are those which can be reduced to calculation problems by the process of some reasoning. Some adequate training enables children to calculate with the abacus much faster than with the traditional means of pencil and paper. So abacus experts are of opinion that, taking into consideration the time spent on practice for learning abacus operation, the abacus or "soroban," made good use of in the course of arithmetic, may facilitate teaching and learning arithmetic, to say nothing of its immense utility in business and everyday life.

The final but most remarkable utility of the abacus is that it enables the blind to calculate much more rapidly than the sighted who calculate with pencil and paper. In Japanese schools for the blind, all kinds of instruments for aid to calculation by the blind have, hitherto, been introduced only to be discarded soon for the abacus, which has proved by far the most effective instrument for teaching the ideas of numbers and mathematics to blind children. In Japan an abacus grading examination for blind children was initiated in 1964 by the Chamber of Commerce and Industry. Today we have reasons to expect that a world-wide examination for blind children will be instituted under the joint sponsorship of the Pan-East Asian Abacus Association of Japan, South Korea, and Taiwan; and the newer abacus associations of the U. S., Europe, Mexico, and other countries.

II. BRIEF HISTORY OF THE ABACUS

The imperfect numerical notation and the scarcity of suitable writing materials in ancient times are presumed to have given rise to the need for devices of mechanical calculation. While the definite origin of the abacus is obscure, there is some reason for believing that its earliest form was a reckoning table covered with sand or fine dust, in which figures were drawn with a stylus, to be erased with the finger when necessary. The English word *abacus* is etymologically derived from the Greek *abax*, meaning a reckoning table covered with dust, which in turn comes from a Semitic word meaning dust or a reckoning table covered with dust or sand. In time this sand-dust abacus gave place to a ruled table upon which counters or disks were arranged on lines to indicate numbers. Various forms of this line abacus were in common use in Europe until the opening of the seventeenth century. In rather remote times, a third form of abacus appeared in certain parts of the world. Instead of lines on which loose counters were laid, the table had movable counters sliding up and down grooves.

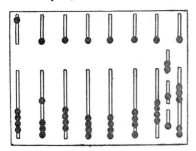

ROMAN GROOVED ABACUS

All three types of abacuses were found at some time or other in ancient Rome – the dust abacus, the line abacus, and the grooved abacus. Out of this last type yet a fourth form of the abacus was developed—one with beads sliding on rods fixed in a frame. This form, the bead or rod abacus, with which calculations can be made much more quickly than on paper, is still used in China, Japan, and other parts of the world. In Europe, after the introduction of Arabic numerals, instrumental arithmetic ceased to make much progress and finally gave way altogether to the graphical as the supply of writing materials became gradually abundant.

As for the Orient, a form of the counting-rod abacus, called *ch'eou* in China and *sangi* in Japan, had been used since ancient times as a means of calculation. The Chinese abacus itself seems, according to the best evidence, to have originated in Central or Western Asia. There is a sixth-century Chinese reference to an abacus on which counters were rolled in grooves. The description of this ancient Chinese abacus and the known intercourse between East and West give us good reason to believe that the Chinese abacus was suggested by the Roman. The Chinese write in vertical columns from above downwards. If they ever are compelled to write in a horizontal line, they write from right to left. But the abacus is worked from left to right. This is another indication that the abacus was not indigenous to China. The present Chinese bead abacus, which is generally called *suan-pan* (arithmetic board) in Mandarin and *soo-pan* in the southern dialect, was a later development, probably appearing in the twelfth century, and did not come into common use till the fourteenth century. It is only natural that the people of the Orient, having retained a system of numerical notation unsuited for calculation, should have developed the abacus to a high degree, and its continuous universal use even after the introduction of Arabic numerals is eloquent testimony to the great efficiency achieved in its development.

The Japanese word for abacus, *soroban*, is probably the Japanese rendering of the Chinese *suan-pan*. Although the *soroban* did not come into popular use in Japan until the seventeenth century, there is no doubt that it must have been known to Japanese merchants at least a couple of centuries earlier. In any case, once this convenient instrument of calculation became widely known in Japan, it was studied extensively and intensively by many mathematicians, including Seki Kowa (1640—1708), who discovered a native calculus independent of the Newtonian theory. As a result of all this study, the form and operational methods of the abacus have undergone one improvement after another. Like the present-day Chinese *suan-pan*, the *soroban* long had two beads above the beam and five below. But toward the close of the nineteenth century it was simplified by reducing the two beads above the beam to one, and finally around 1920 it acquired its present shape by omitting yet another bead, reducing those below the beam from five to four.

Thus the present form of the *soroban* is a crystalization of labor and ingenuity in the field of Oriental mathematics and science. We feel sure that the *soroban*, enjoying widespread use in this mechanical age on account of its distinct advantages over the lightning calculating machine, will continue to be used in the coming atomic age as well.

III. BASIC PRINCIPLES OF CALCULATION

The abacus is a simple instrument for performing rapid arithmetical calculation. It consists of an oblong wooden frame or board holding a number of vertically arranged rods, on which wooden beads, balls, or counters slide up and down. A beam running across the board divides the rods into two sections : upper and lower. The most common type of abacus in Japan has twenty-one bamboo rods, and is about twelve inches long by two inches wide. But larger types with twenty-seven or thirty-one rods, and smaller ones with seventeen or thirteen rods, are also used. As described at the conclusion of the preceding chapter, and as may be seen in the accompanying illustration, the number of beads per rod has been progressively reduced, in the interests of simplicity and ease of operation, from seven to six, and finally to five. Until recently an abacus with five beads in the lower section of each rod was in general use. But this type of abacus has now been largely replaced by a one with four beads on each rod below the beam.

The abacus is based on the decimal system. For convenience in cal-

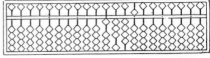

FIG. 1. MODERN JAPANESE ABACUS

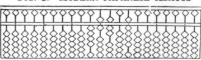

FIG. 2. OLDER-TYPE JAPANESE ABACUS

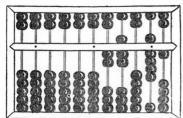

FIG. 3. MODERN CHINESE ABACUS

culation the beam is marked with a unit point at every third rod. These unit points serve to indicate the decimal point and other units of decimal measure. For example, select any rod near the center of the board which is marked with a unit point, and call this the unit rod of the problem. Then the first rod to its left is the tens' rod, the second is the hundreds' rod, the third rod (marked with another unit point) is the thousands' rod, etc. On the other hand, the first rod to the right of the unit rod is the tenths', the second is the hundredths', the third (likewise marked with another point) is the thousandths' rod, etc.

Each of the four beads on the lower section of a rod has the value of 1, while the bead on the upper section of a rod has the value of 5. Each of the 1-unit beads below the beam obtains its value when it is moved up toward the beam, and loses its value when it is moved back down to its former position. On the other hand, each of the 5-unit beads above the beam obtains its value when it is moved down to the beam and loses its value when it is moved back up.

The beads in Figure 1, using the third unit point from the right to designate the unit rod, represent the number 1,345, while Figure 2 shows 46,709.

Before using the abacus, make sure that all the beads are in the neutral position representing zero. This is done by moving up all 5-unit beads and moving down all 1-unit beads. In clearing the abacus for use, hold the left end with your left middle finger on its upper edge and your left thumb on its lower edge, and move all beads down by slanting the upper edge toward your body. After leveling the abacus again, raise all 5-unit beads by moving the right index finger from left to right along the upper edge of the beam.

When calculating on the abacus, use two fingers : the right index finger and thumb. Some operators use only the index finger, but experiments show that it is more efficient to use the thumb as well. Nearly all experts use two fingers. Use the index finger to move 5-units beads up and down and to move 1-unit beads down, while using the thumb only to move 1-unit beads up. For instance, to place the figure 7 on the abacus with only the index finger requires two successive motions— first move down a 5-unit bead, and then move up two 1-unit beads—whereas these motions can be performed simultaneously with two fingers, with a corresponding increase in efficiency.

Moreover, in our everyday actions we commonly employ two or more fingers, say in picking up something or in holding a pen, and the hand is so made that the index finger almost always requires the assistance of the thumb. This accounts for the proven fact that, in the long run, it is much less tiring to operate the abacus with two fingers than with but one.

Experiments also show that the index finger can move beads down more quickly and accurately than the thumb, while on the other hand the thumb can move beads up with greater speed, force, and accuracy than the index finger.

The best and quickest way to acquire skill in abacus manipulation is to use the index finger and thumb in strict accord with the prescribed rules for bead manipulation. The correct finger movements will be indicated in detail for a number of problems in the next chapter. They should·be carefully heeded and practised many times until you can flick your two fingers as nimbly and effortlessly as the fingers of a pianist glide over the keys in executing a sonata.

Another important secret for acquiring rapid skill in abacus calculation is always to keep your fingers close to the beads. Never raise your fingers high from the beads nor put them deep between the beads. Glide the beads up and down by touching their ridges just slightly with the tips of your fingers.

The guiding principles for the movement of beads, as followed hereafter, may be summarized thus :

General Rules for Moving Beads

1. Move down a 5-unit bead and move up one or more 1-unit beads at the same time. (See Example 5, next chapter.)
2. First move down one or more 1-unit beads, and then move up a 5-unit bead. (See Example 6.)
3. In quick succession first move down a 5-unit bead, and then one or more 1-unit beads. (See Examples 7 and 9.)
4. In quick succession first move up one or more 1-unit beads, and then a 5-unit bead. (See Examples 8 and 9.)
5. In addition, after finishing operation on the unit rod, move up a 1-unit bead on the tens' rod. (See Examples 11, 13, 15, 17 and 19.)
6. In subtraction, after subtracting a 1-unit bead from the tens' rod, operate on the unit rod. (See Examples 12, 14, 16,

FIG. 4

18 and 20.)

When working with the abacus, sit up straight at a desk. A good posture will have much to do with the speed and accuracy of your calculations.

Finally, in studying the illustrations which accompany the examples given throughout the rest of the book, the following key should be kept in mind:

Key to Illustrations

1. A white bead ($\Diamond$) is one which is in its original position and has no numerical value.
2. A striped bead (⬙) is one which has just been moved, thereby having either obtained or lost its numerical value.
3. A black bead ($\blacklozenge$) is one which obtained numerical value in a previous step.
4. $\downarrow$ indicates that beads are to be moved down with the index finger.
5. $\uparrow$ indicates that beads are to be moved up with the index finger.
6. δ indicates that beads are to be moved up with the thumb.
7. Figures in parentheses accompanying the foregoing signs indicate the order in which beads are to be moved.

IV. ADDITION AND SUBTRACTION

There are four principal arithmetical calculations on the abacus : addition, subtraction, multiplication, and division. Of these, addition and subtraction are basic processes, for unless you know how to add and subtract on the abacus, you cannot multiply or divide. In our daily life and business accounts, addition is used far more frequently than the other processes and is most important of all.

The central part of the abacus is generally used for addition and subtraction. However, when many large numbers are to be added, the first number is set at the right side of the abacus, because the working extends to the left. In any case a one-digit number and the last digit of a larger number should always be set on a unit rod, that is, on a rod marked with a unit point.

1. Adding and Subtracting One-Digit Numbers

Example 1. 1+2=3

Step 1 : Set the number 1 by moving up one 1-unit bead with the thumb (Fig. 5). See that you set 1 on a unit rod marked with a unit point.

Step 2 : Add 2 to 1 by moving up, on the same rod, two more 1-unit beads, using the

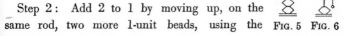

FIG. 5   FIG. 6

thumb (Fig. 6).

Note 1: This example illustrates the procedure used in adding one or more 1-unit beads. The problems to which this procedure applies are:

1+1	2+1	3+1	5+1	6+1	7+1	8+1
1+2	2+2		5+2	6+2	7+2	
1+3			5+3	6+3		
			5+4			

Note 2: Hereafter, such phrases as "move up one 1-unit bead," "move down three 1-unit beads," etc., will be shortened to "set 1," "move down 3," etc.

Example 2. 3−2=1

Step 1: Set 3 with the thumb (Fig. 7).

Step 2: Subtract 2 by moving down two 1-unit beads with the index finger (Fig. 8).

Note: This example illustrates the procedure

FIG. 7 FIG. 8   used in subtracting one or more 1-unit beads. The problems to which this procedure applies are:

2−1	3−1	4−1	6−1	7−1	8−1	9−1
	3−2	4−2		7−2	8−2	9−2
		4−3			8−3	9−3
						9−4

Example 3. 2+5=7

Step 1: Set 2 (Fig. 9).

Step 2: Move down 5 with the index finger (Fig. 10).

Note: This example illustrates the procedure

FIG. 9 FIG. 10   used in adding a 5-unit bead. The problems to which this procedure applies are:

1+5	2+5	3+5	4+5

Example 4. $7-5=2$

Step 1: Set 7 (Fig. 11).

Step 2: Move up 5 with the index finger (Fig. 12).

FIG. 11   FIG. 12

Note: This example shows the procedure used in subtracting a 5-unit bead. The problems to which this procedure are:

5−5	6−5	8−5	9−5

Example 5. $2+6=8$

Step 1: Set 2 (Fig. 13).

Step 2: Move down 5 with the index finger and move up 1 with the thumb at the same time (Fig. 14).

FIG. 13   FIG. 14

Note: This example illustrates the procedure used in adding both a 5-unit bead and one or more 1-unit beads. The problems to which this procedure applies are:

1+6	2+6	3+6
1+7	2+7	
1+8		

Example 6. $8-6=2$

Step 1: Set 8 (Fig. 15).

Step 2: After moving down 1 with the index finger, move up 5 with the same finger (Fig. 16).

FIG. 15   FIG. 16

Note 1: This example shows how to subtract both one or more 1-unit beads and a 5-unit bead. The problems to which this procedure applies are:

9−9	9−8	9−7	9−6
	8−8	8−7	8−6
		7−7	7−6
			6−6

Note 2 : The above-mentioned procedure is preferable to moving up 5 first and 1 next with the index finger. As is explained in Note 2 of Example 15, in some cases the latter procedure makes it difficult to move the fingers nimbly, e. g., the addition of 4 to 9.

Example 7. 4+1=5

FIG. 17 FIG. 18 FIG. 19

Step 1 : Set 4 (Fig. 17).

Step 2 : Move down 5 first and 4 next in close succession with the index finger (Fig. 18).

Note 1 : This example illustrates the procedure used in setting 5 when the addition of two numbers makes 5. The problems to which this procedure applies are:

4+1	3+2	2+3	1+4

Note 2 : Fig. 19 illustrates the incorrect way to perform Step 2. Note that the correct way (Fig. 18) requires but a single continuing down stroke of the finger whereas the incorrect way requires three separate movements: (1) move down 4, (2) move the finger back up, and (3) move down 5, resulting in a loss of time and effort. (See Notes 2 and 3 of Example 9.)

Example 8. 5−1=4

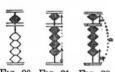

FIG. 20 FIG. 21 FIG. 22

Step 1 : Set 5 (Fig. 20).

Step 2 : First move up 4 with the thumb, and then move up 5 with the index finger in close succession (Fig. 21). Flick the thumb and the index finger with the idea of performing the two motions at the same time.

Note 1 : This example illustrates the procedure of subtracting a number from 5. The problems to which this procedure applies are:

5 − 1,	5 − 2,	5 − 3,	5 − 4
	6 − 2,	6 − 3,	6 − 4
		7 − 3,	7 − 4
			8 − 4

Note 2 : As explained in Step 2 of this example, when 1 is subtracted from 5, four 1-unit beads and one 5-unit bead should be pushed up at the same time. But if the beginner finds it hard to make the two motions at the same time, he may perform each separately by first pushing up four 1-unit beads, and then a 5-unit bead (Fig. 21).

Fig. 22 illustrates the incorrect way to perform Step 2. Note that the correct way requires but a single continuous up stroke of the thumb and the index finger, whereas the incorrect way requires three separate movements. This means that your finger or at least your attention has to travel further, resulting in a loss of time and effort.

Example 9. 4 + 3 = 7

Step 1 : Set 4 (Fig. 23).

Step 2 : First move down 5, and then 2 in close succession with the index finger (Fig. 24).

Fig. 23 Fig. 24

Note 1 : This example illustrates the procedure used in adding a 5-unit bead and subtracting one or more 1-unit beads. The problems to which this procedure applies :

4 + 1	4 + 2	4 + 3	4 + 4
	3 + 2	3 + 3	3 + 4
		2 + 3	2 + 4
			1 + 4

Note 2 : Since three 1-unit beads cannot be added to the four 1-unit beads, 5 is added and 2 is subtracted to offset the excess. This operation may be represented in the form of the equation : $4 + 3 = 4 + (5 - 2) = 7$

Note 3 : When working the foregoing example, do not think: Since 3 plus 4 equals 7, I must form 7 on the board. Instead, simply remember that 2 is the complementary digit with which 3 makes 5, and by flicking down 5 and 2 in rapid succession, allow the sum 7 to form itself naturally on the board. There are only two groups of complementary digits for 5: 3 and 2, and 4 and 1. Operation by means of complementary digits is much simpler and less liable to error than the ordinary mode of calculation. For further explanation of calculation by means of complementary digits, see Note 3 to Example 20.

Example 10. $7 - 3 = 4$

Step 1 : Set 7   (Fig. 25).

Step 2 : In close succession, first move up 2 with the thumb, and then move up the 5 with the index finger with the idea of performing

FIG. 25 FIG. 26   the two motions at the same time   (Fig. 26).

Note 1 : This example illustrates the procedure for adding one or more 1-unit beads and subtracting one 5-unit bead. Problems to which applicable :

5 − 1	5 − 2	5 − 3	5 − 4
	6 − 2	6 − 3	6 − 4
		7 − 3	7 − 4
			8 − 4

Note 2 : Since three 1-unit beads cannot be subtracted from the two 1-unit beads, 2 is added and 5 is subtracted   This operation may be represented by the equation :

$$7 - 3 = 7 + 2 - 5 = 4$$

Note 3 : When working this example, do not think: 3 from 7 leaves 4, so 4 must be formed on the board. Instead, simply remember that 2 is the complementary digit with which 3 makes 5, and allow the result to form itself naturally on the board.   (See Note 3 to Example 20.)

Example 11. $3 + 7 = 10$

Step 1: Set 3 on a unit rod, which we shall call B (Fig. 27).

Step 2: In close succession, first move down then 3 on B with the index finger, and then move up 1 on the tens' rod, here called A, with the thumb (Fig. 28). Flick the index finger and the thumb in a twisting manner so that you may perform the two motions at the same time.

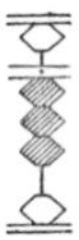

B A B

FIG. 27 FIG. 28

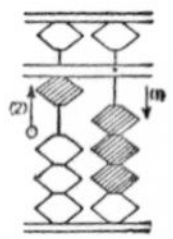

Note 1: This example shows how to set 10 when it is the sum of two digits. This procedure requires the subtraction of one or more 1-unit beads. Problems to which applicable:

1+9	2+8	3+7	4+6

Note 2: In working out this example, do not move up 1 on the tens' rod until you have moved down 3 on the unit rod B. If you follow this incorrect procedure, you will never improve in bead calculation. For the theoretical reasons for the advantages of the correct procedure, see Note 5 (The Order of Operation) to Example 20.

Example 12. $10 - 7 = 3$

Step 1: Set 10. This is done by simply moving up one bead on the tens' rod A (Fig. 29).

Step 2: First remove the 10 by moving down the 1 on the tens' rod A with the index finger, and then move up 3 on the unit rod B with the thumb (Fig. 30).

A B A B

FIG. 29 FIG. 30

Note 1: This example shows how to subtract 10 and add one or more 1-unit beads. Problems to which such procedure applies:

| 10−9 | 10−8 | 10−7 | 10−6 |

Note 2: In working out this example, be sure to move down 1 on the tens' rod A before moving up 3 on the unit rod B. For the theoretical reasons for the advantages of the correct procedure, see Note 5 (The Order of Operation) to Example 20.

Example 13. 6+4=10

A B   A B
Fig. 31   Fig. 32

Step 1: Set 6 on the unit rod B.

Step 2: Move down 1 on B with the index finger, then move up 5 on B with the same finger, and finally move up 1 on on the tens' rod A with the thumb. Work the index finger and the thumb with the idea of performing the last two motions at the same time.

Note: This example shows how to form the sum 10 when it is made by the addition of two digits. This procedure, requiring the subtraction of both one or more 1-unit beads and a 5-unit bead, applies to the problems:

| 6+4 | 7+3 | 8+2 | 9+1 |

Example 14. 10−4=6

A B   A B
Fig. 33   Fig. 34

Step 1: Set 1 on the tens' rod A.

Step 2: First move down the 1 on A with the index finger, then move down 5 and move up 1 on B at the same time.

Note: This example shows how to subtract 10 and add both a 5-unit bead and one or more 1-unit beads. Applicable problems:

| 10−4 | 10−3 | 10−2 | 10−1 |

Example 15. 9+4=13

Step 1: Set 9 on the unit rod B.

Step 2: Move down 1 on B with the index finger, then move up 5 on B with the same finger and finally move up 1 on A with the thumb. Work the index finger and the thumb with the idea of performing the last two motions at the same time.

A B   A B

Fig. 35   Fig. 36

Note 1: This example shows how to add 10 after subtracting one or more 1-unit beads and a 5-unit bead. Applicable problems:

9+1	9+2	9+3	9+4
	8+2	8+3	8+4
		7+3	7+4
			6+4

Note 2: Do not reverse motions 1 and 2 of Step 2. If you do, your operation will slow down. Because after moving up 5, you will find it hard to move down 1 on B and move up 1 on A at the same time in the manner of twisting your fingers, although this latter procedure is workable in some cases, for example, in adding 4 to 6 or 7. This is the main reason why experts, in working out Example 6 ($8-6=2$), disfavor the procedure of moving up 5 first, and moving down 1 next.

Example 16. $13-4=9$

Step 1: Set 13 on AB.

Step 2: After moving down the 1 on A, move down 5 and move up 1 on B at the same time.

A B   A B

Fig. 37   Fig. 38

Note: This example shows how to add both a 5-unit bead and one or more 1-unit bead after subtracting 10. Applicable problems.

11-2	11-3	11-4
	12-3	12-4
		13-4

Example 17 6+6=12

A B   A B
FIG. 39   FIG. 40

Step 1 : Set 6 on the unit rod B.

Step 2 : Move up 1 on B (Motion 1), move up 5 on B (Motion 2), and move up 1 on A (Motion 3). Work the two fingers with the idea of performing the first two motions at the same time.

Note 1 : This example shows how to add 1 to the tens' rod after adding one or more 1-unit beads and subtracting a 5-unit bead on the unit rod. Applicable problems :

5+6	6+6	7+6	8+6
5+7	6+7	7+7	
5+8	6+8		
5+9			

A B   A B
FIG. 41   FIG. 42

Note 2 : It is possible to perform the last two motions of Step 2 above at the same time after completing the first motion. But this procedure should not be followed, as it does not work in some cases. For example, the problem, " 46+6=52 " (Figs. 41 and 42) or " 96+6=102," can be worked in no other way than that indicated.

Example 18 12−6=6

A B   A B
FIG. 43   FIG. 44

Step 1 : Set 12 on AB.

Step 2 : After moving down the 1 on A, move down 5 and 1 on B in succession.

Note: This example shows how to add a 5-unit bead and subtract one or more 1-unit beads after subtracting 10. Applicable problems :

11−6			
12−6	12−7		
13−6	13−7	13−8	
14−6	14−7	14−8	14−9

Example 19. $9+7=16$

Step 1: Set 9 on the unit rod B.

Step 2: Move down 3 on B, and move up 1 on A. Perform the two motions mechanically at the same time as if twisting the thumb and the index finger.

A B   A B

FIG. 45   FIG. 46

Note 1: This example shows how to subtract one or more 1-unit beads from the unit rod and add 10. Applicable problems:

2+9	3+9	4+9	6+9	7+9	8+9	9+9
	3+8	4+8		7+8	8+8	9+8
		4+7			8+7	9+7
						9+6

Note 2: Since 7 cannot be added to the 9 on the unit rod B, 3, the complementary digit of 7 for 10, is subtracted and 10 is added. This operation may be represented by the equation:

$$9+7=9-3+10=16$$

Example 20. $16-7=9$

Step 1: Set 16 on AB.

Step 2: Move down the 1 on A, and move up 3 on B.

Note 1: When setting a two-digit number on the board, as in Step 1, always set the tens' digit first.

A B   A B

FIG. 47   FIG. 48

Note 2: This example shows how to subtract 10 and add one or more 1-unit beads. Applicable problems:

15−6	15−7	15−8	15−9
	16−7	16−8	16−9
		17−8	17−9
			18−9

Note 3: Since 7 cannot be subtracted from the 6 on the

unit rod, 10 is subtracted from rod A, and 3, the complementary digit of 7 for 10, is added. The basis for this operation may be represented by the equation :

$$16-7=16-10+3=9$$

Note 4 : Mechanization of Operation.

The fundamental principle which makes abacus operation simple and speedy is mechanization. To give a theoretical explanation, the mechanical operation of the abacus is designed to minimize your mental labor and limit it to the unit rod, without carrying it to the tens' rod, by means of the complementary digits for 10 and 5, and to let the result form itself mechanically and naturally on the board.

To give an example, in adding 7 to 9, the student accustomed to the Western mode of calculation will probably form 16 on the board as a result of mental calculation to the effect that 9 and 7 is 16. But such procedure is in every way inferior to the above-mentioned mechanical one. Not only does this Western method require mental exertion and time but it is liable to cause perplexity and errors.

When a problem of addition and subtraction is worked on the board, the procedure is very simple. Addition and subtraction, which involve two rods, are simplified by means of a complementary digit, that is, the digit necessary to give the sum 10 when added to a given digit. For instance, suppose we have to add 7 on a rod where there is 9 ; then we think or say, " 7 and 3 is 10," and subtract 3 from the rod in question, and add 1 to next rod on the left. When we have to subtract 7 from 16, we think or say, " 7 from 10 leaves 3," and subtract 1 from the next rod on the left, and add 3 to the rod in question. This means that 10 is always reduced to 1, and added or subtracted on the tens' rod. Therefore, after recalling the complementary digit, the operator has simply to perform either of the two mechanical operations: subtracting the complementary digit and adding 1 on the tens' rod (in addition) or subtracting 1 on the tens' rod and adding the complementary digit (in subtraction). The result then will naturally form on the board. No matter how many digits may be contained in the numbers to be added or subtracted, the entire operation is performed by applying this mechanical method to each digit in turn.

The same mechanical method applies to the operations which require the analysis of 5 (see Examples 7 to 10). Suppose we have to add 3 to 4; then we merely think of the complementary digit of 3 for 5 (that is, the digit necessary to give the sum 5 when added to 3), and we move down the 5-unit digit and two 1-unit digits on the rod in question. Then the result will naturally appear on the board. Any attempt to calculate the answer mentally will retard the operation.

10 has only five groups of complementary digits: 9 and 1, 8 and 2, 7 and 3, 6 and 4, and 5 and 5, while 5 has only two: 4 and 1, and 3 and 2. Accordingly, the use of the mechanized method requires no more mental effort than that of remembering one of the elements of each of these very few pairs of complementary digits. This is the fundamental reason which makes calculation by means of the complementary digit much simpler and speedier and less liable to error than the ordinary way of mental or written calculation.

The following examples will show how much more laborious the ordinary calculation is. In written calculation we proceed from right to left. For instance in the problem $99 + 88 + 77 + 66$, we first add the unit digits, thinking "$9 + 8 = 17$, $17 + 7 = 24$, and $24 + 6 = 30$." Next we add the 30 to the 90 of 99 and work on. In the problem $567 - 89$, we cannot subtract the 9 from 7, so borrowing 10 from the 6 in the tens' place, we get 8. Next proceeding to the tens' place we again find that we cannot subtract the 8 from the remaining 5 of the minuend, so we borrow 1 from the remaining 5 in the hundreds' place, and we get 7 in the tens' place and the answer 478. These processes involve laborious mental exertion.

On the other hand, all calculations on the abacus proceed from left to right, that is, from the highest to the lowest digit. This accords with our natural customary practice of naming or remembering all numbers from the highest to the lowest digit. Therefore, to set numbers on the board is to calculate numbers.

In conclusion, incredibly speedy abacus operation is mainly attributable to three reasons: mechanical operation by means of the complementary digit, left to right operation, and the previously explained dozen rules of rational or scientific bead manipulation. These are the reasons why, no matter how rapidly numbers may be mentioned, as long as they are given distinctly, the skilled abacus operator can add and subtract without any error, irrespective of how many digits the numbers may contain.

Note 5 : The Order of Operation.

When addition involves two rods, as in the example $9+7=16$, be sure to subtract 3 from the unit rod, and next add 10 in the form of 1 to the tens' rod. Thus $9+7=9-3+10=16$.

The idea of 7 in the terms of the complementary digit is " $7=10-3$." So you would be tempted to add 10 first and subtract 3 next. But as already pointed out, such a procedure which involves unnecessary shifts of attention between the unit rod and the tens' rod, should not be followed. Because in adding 7 to 9, you will naturally first observe the unit rod to add 7. Now subtract 3 from the unit rod, and then, proceeding to the tens' rod, add 1. This procedure requires only two shifts of attention and operation. On the other hand, if you did not subtract 3 first, you would have to come back to the unit rod to subtract 3 after adding 1 to the tens' rod. This inferior procedure would delay your operation.

The advantage of the correct procedure becomes even clearer in some problems containing more than one digit. For instance, in adding 7 to 996, note the decided advantage of forming 3 and proceeding mechanically straight to the left to clear the tens' and hundreds' rods of their 9 and to set 1 on the thousands', as shown in Figs. 49 and 50.

A B C D
FIG. 49

A B C D
FIG. 50

When subtraction involves two rods, as in the example $15 - 7 = 8$, be sure to subtract 10 in the form of 1 from the tens' rod, and next add 3 to the unit rod. Thus

$$15 - 7 = 15 - 10 + 3 = 8.$$

In subtracting 7, naturally you will first look at the unit rod; then you will see that it is impossible to subtract 7 from 6 and that you must borrow 10 from the tens' rod. At this instant subtract 10 in the form of 1, and then add 3, i. e., the complementary digit of 7 for 10, to the unit rod. So following this natural order of attention, first subtract the 10 and then add the 3. If you were to reverse this order, you would have to shift your attention back again to the tens' rod to subtract 10 after adding 3. Thus this wrong procedure would cause needless shifting of attention and delay operation. Note that failure to use the complementary digit would necessitate the less efficient method of mental calculation.

The correct procedure is especially advantageous in some problems containing more than one digit, e.g., the problem

$$1,000 - 1 = 999.$$

Following the correct procedure, in this problem we can proceed mechanically straight from left to right (Fig. 52), while the incorrect procedure (Fig. 53) involves the loss of time and labor.

A B C D
FIG. 51

A B C D
FIG. 52

A B C D
FIG. 53

When setting numbers of two or more digits, set the tens' first. Also, when adding or subtracting numbers of two or more digits, add or subtract beginning with the highest-place digit. This is another fundamental rule which will produce efficiency. As previously explained, when a number is named or given, beginning with the highest digit, it can be mentally remembered or set and calculated much more naturally and easily on the board than beginning with the lowest digit. This method is opposite to that of written calculation, which is started backward with the last digit after a number has been given.

2. Adding and Subtracting Two-Digit Numbers

When setting two-digit numbers, set the tens' first. Also when adding and subtracting two-digit numbers, add and subtract the tens' first. On the abacus always operate from left to right. This is a fundamental rule based on efficiency. The efficiency of this rule is especially true in the calculation of large numbers, as in Examples 26 and 27. As explained in the introduction, since a number is named or given, beginning with the highest digit, it can be mentally remembered or set and calculated much more naturally and easily on the board, beginning with the highest-place digit than with the lowest-place. Written calculation is started backward with the last digit after a number has been given, whereas on the abacus a number is calculated while it is being given, in other words, to set a number is to calculate it.

Example 21. $14+25=39$

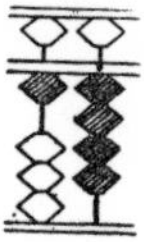

A B	
·	
1 4	Step 1
+ 2	Step 2
3 4	Result of Step 2
+ 5	Step 3
3 9	Result of Step 3

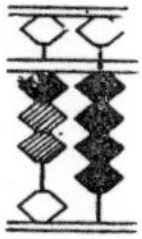

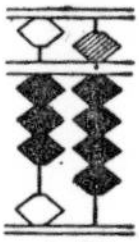

A B   A B   A B
FIG. 54   FIG. 55   FIG. 56

Step 1:   Set 14 on AB, with the 4 appearing on the unit rod B   (Fig. 54).

Step 2:   Add the 2 of 25 to the 1 on A with the thumb. This gives 3 on A and 34 on AB   (Fig. 55).

Step 3:   Add the remaining 5 of 25 to the 4 on B with the forefinger.   This gives 9 on B. The answer is 39   (Fig. 56).

The same procedure can be expressed diagramatically as seen above.

Example 22. $45+27=72$

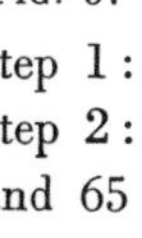

A B	
·	
4 5	Step 1
+ 2	Step 2
6 5	
+ 7	Step 3
7 2	

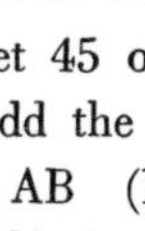

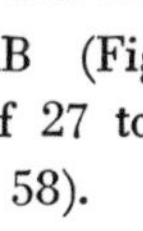

A B   A B   A B
FIG. 57   FIG. 58   FIG. 59

Step 1:   Set 45 on AB   (Fig. 57).

Step 2:   Add the 2 of 27 to the 4 on A. This gives 6 on A and 65 on AB   (Fig. 58).

Step 3:   Add the remaining 7 of 27 to the 5 on B.   This gives 2 on B and 7 on A, as 1 is carried to the 6 on A. The answer is 72   (Fig. 59).

Example 23 $79-23=56$

Step 1:   Set 79 on AB   (Fig. 60).

Step 2 : Subtract the 2 of 23 from the 7 on A. This

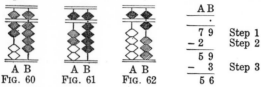

A B	
·	
7 9	Step 1
− 2	Step 2
5 9	
− 3	Step 3
5 6	

A B · · · A B · · · A B
FIG. 60 · · FIG. 61 · · FIG. 62

leaves 5 on A and 59 on AB (Fig. 61).

Step 3 : Subtract the remaining 3 of 23 from the 9 on B.
This leaves 6 on B. The answer is 56   (Fig. 62).

Example 24. $83-49=34$

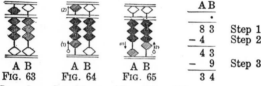

A B	
·	
8 3	Step 1
− 4	Step 2
4 3	
− 9	Step 3
3 4	

A B · · · A B · · · A B
FIG. 63 · · FIG. 64 · · FIG. 65

Step 1 : Set 83 on AB   (Fig. 63).

Step 2 : Subtract the 4 of 49 from the 8 on A. This
leaves 4 on A and 43 on AB   (Fig. 64).

Step 3 : Subtract the remaining 9 of 49 from the 3 on B.
As you cannot subtract 9 from 3, borrow 1 from A This
leaves 3 on A and enables you to subtract 9 from 10 on B.
Add, to the 3 on B, the remainder 1 of 9 from 10, and you
get 4 on B. The answer is 34   (Fig. 65).

3. Adding and Subtracting Numbers of Over Two Digits

The methods used in adding or subtracting numbers containing
three or more digits are the same as those just described in
the case of two-digit numbers. Two problems each in addition
and subtraction will suffice to make this clear.

Example 25. $456+789=1,245$

Step 1 : Set 456 on BCD   (Fig. 66).

Step 2 : Add the 7 of 789 to the 4 on B. This gives you

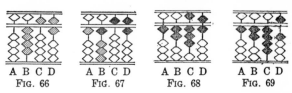

A B C D	A B C D	A B C D	A B C D
Fig. 66	Fig. 67	Fig. 68	Fig. 69

A B C D	
· ·	
4 5 6	Step 1
+ 7	Step 2
1, 1 5 6	
+ 8	Step 3
1, 2 3 6	
+ 9	Step 4
1, 2 4 5	

is 1245.

11 on AB and 1,156 on ABCD   (Fig. 67).

Step 3: Add the 8 of the remaining 89 to the 5 on C. This gives you 23 on BC and 1,236 on ABCD   (Fig. 68).

Step 4: Add the remaining 9 to the 6 on D. This gives you 45 on CD. The answer is 1,245   (Fig. 69).

Example 26. $3,179 + 5,876 = 9,055$

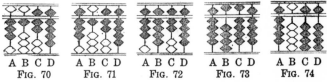

A B C D	A B C D	A B C D	A B C D	A B C D
Fig. 70	Fig. 71	Fig. 72	Fig. 73	Fig. 74

A B C D	
· ·	
3, 1 7 9	Step 1
+ 5	Step 2
8, 1 7 9	
+ 8	Step 3
8, 9 7 9	
+ 7	Step 4
9, 0 4 9	
+ 6	Step 5
9, 0 5 5	

Step 1: Set 3,179 on ABCD   (Fig. 70).

Step 2: Add the 5 of 5,876 to the 3 on A. This gives you 8 on A and 8,179 on ABCD.

Step 3: Add the 8 of the remaining 876 to the 1 on B. This gives you 9 on B and 8,979 on ABCD   (Fig. 72).

Step 4: Add the 7 of the remaining 76 to the 7 on C. This gives you 904 on ABC and 9,049 on ABCD   (Fig. 73).

Step 5: Add the remaining 6 to the 9 on D. This gives you 55 on CD. The answer is 9,055   (Fig. 74).

Example 27. $623 - 375 = 248$

Step 1: Set 623 on ABC   (Fig. 75).

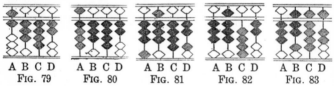

A B C	
·	
6 2 3	Step 1
− 3	Step 2
3 2 3	
− 7	Step 3
2 5 3	
− 5	Step 4
2 4 8	

A B C — FIG. 75 A B C — FIG. 76 A B C — FIG. 77 A B C — FIG. 78

Step 2: Subtract the 3 of 375 from the 6 on A. This leaves 3 on A and 323 on ABC (Fig. 76).

Step 3: Subtract the 7 of the remaining 75 from the 2 on B by borrowing 1 from the 3 on A. This leaves 25 on AB and 253 on ABC (Fig. 77).

Step 4: Subtract the remaining 5 from the 3 on C by borrowing 1 from the 5 on B. This leaves 48 on BC. The answer is 248 (Fig. 78).

Example 28. 6,342−2,547=3,795

A B C D — FIG. 79 A B C D — FIG. 80 A B C D — FIG. 81 A B C D — FIG. 82 A B C D — FIG. 83

A B C D	
· ·	
6,3 4 2	Step 1
− 2	Step 2
4,3 4 2	
− 5	Step 3
3,8 4 2	
− 4	Step 4
3,8 0 2	
− 7	Step 5
3,7 9 5	

Step 1: Set 6,342 on ABCD, with 6 on the thousands' rod and 2 on the ones' (Fig. 79).

Step 2: Subtract the 2 of 2,547 from the 6 on A. This leaves 4 on A and 4,342 on ABCD (Fig. 80).

Step 3: Subtract the 5 of the remaining 547 from the 3 on B by borrowing 1 from the 4 on A. This leaves 38 on AB and 3,842 on ABCD (Fig. 81).

Step 4: Subtract the 4 of the remaining 47 from the 4 on

C. This leaves 0 on C on 3,802 on ABCD (Fig. 82).

Step 5: Subtract the remaining 7 from the 2 on D by borrowing 1 from the 8 on B. This leaves 795 on BCD. The answer is 3,795 (Fig. 83).

4. Exercises

Probably the most convenient way of dealing with problems containing a long file of numbers, such as the following, is to use the top edge of the abacus as a marker. For example, in problem 1 on page 52, first place the top edge of the abacus immediately under the first number, 24, and form it on the board (Fig. 84); then move the abacus down until the next number, 20, appears right above

FIG. 84   FIG. 85

the beard, and add that number on the beads (Fig. 85); and continue in this fashion to the end of the problem.

Abacus calculation is also greatly facilitated by having someone call out the successive numbers. Numbers should be read distinctly and quickly. For example, the number 123, 456, 789 should be given as " one, two, three million; four, five, six thousand; seven, eight, nine."

The best exercise for attaining skill is to add 123,456,789 nine times. If your sum is correct, it will be 1,111,111,101. Again, add 789 nine times on the rods GHI, with I as the unit rod; next add 456 on DEF nine times; finally add 123 on ABC nine times, and you will get the same sum. Subtract 123,456,789 from 1,111,111,101 nine times, and you will end with zero. These three exercises involve every procedure used in problems of addition and subtraction. A third-grade abacus operator can work each of the three exercises in one minute, and a first-grade operator in thirty seconds.

I. Adding and Subtracting Two-Digit Numbers

(1)	(2)	(3)	(4)	(5)	(6)	(7)	(8)
24	55	22	11	33	55	66	55
20	44	66	44	77	55	44	77
−33	−55	−88	−33	−88	−55	−22	−80
−11	−22	77	44	99	54	33	69
22	55	−66	−22	−88	35	−44	−76
12	−11	55	33	77	−55	55	88
−23	−55	−66	−44	−99	75	−33	−66
11	11	0	33	11	164	99	67

II. Adding and Subtracting Three-Digit Numbers

(1)	(2)	(3)	(4)	(5)
222	345	561	621	158
665	762	259	946	732
778	473	846	−255	−345
555	528	667	428	566
335	981	445	564	444
778	811	778	−392	−657
222	176	289	734	216
889	634	265	855	774
443	367	778	−628	−889
223	189	665	−476	−677
5,110	5,266	5,553	2,397	322

III. Adding and Subtracting Four-Digit Numbers

(1)	(2)	(3)	(4)	(5)
3,627	9,105	2,456	7,081	6,924
1,508	2,746	8,193	5,469	8,570
9,472	1,809	5,647	−2,505	1,439
6,345	5,321	7,038	3,748	−3,268
8,160	4,684	9,825	4,917	−7,015
2,079	3,263	3,741	−6,803	9,847
4,384	5,162	6,580	−6,294	5,192
7,819	7,038	1,269	1,372	2,603
5,623	8,574	4,001	9,620	−3,786
1,950	9,970	9,372	8,135	4,051
50,967	57,672	58,122	24,740	24,557

V. MULTIPLICATION

There are several methods of multiplication on the abacus. The one introduced in the following pages is a recent method which is generally considered the best and is now the standard method taught in grade schools. In describing the method, standard terminology will be used. Thus, for example, in the problem $5 \times 2 = 10$, 5 will be called the multiplicand, 2 the multiplier, and 10 the product.

It is customary to set the multiplicand at the central part of the abacus and the multiplier to the left, leaving two or three rods unused between the two numbers, just enough to separate them clearly but not too widely. The decision of the Abacus Committee in favor of two unused rods will be followed in our problems here.

The method of multiplication used here gives the product immediately to the right of the multiplicand. There is a less favored method which gives the first figure of the product immediately to the left.

The multiplier is very often a smaller number than the multiplicand. The small number is easy to remember, thus saving the time and trouble of constantly referring to it. The experienced abacist often saves even the trouble of setting a small multiplier on the abacus. This is believed to be the reason why the multiplicand is customarily set at the right and the multiplier at the left, although there is nothing particularly objectionable to setting the two numbers in the reverse order.

Although the use of a unit rod marked with a unit point does not have as much bearing in problems of multiplication and division as in addition and subtraction, it does facilitate calculation in many ways. Therefore, in the following problems the unit figure of the multiplicand is set on a unit rod. In the case of the multiplier, however, so long as it is not a fractional number, the unit rod is disregarded and the unit figure is set on the third rod to the left of the multiplicand.

As for the order of setting the multiplicand and the multiplier, since the unit figure of the multiplicand must be set on a unit rod, it is advisable for the beginner to set the multiplicand ahead of the multiplier. It should be noted, however, that experts can locate both the multiplicand and the multiplier at a glance. So they very often set the multiplier ahead of of the multiplicand, thus saving the time required in shifting the hand back to the left after setting the multiplicand. Even more frequently experts set only the multiplicand on the board not even troubling to set the multiplier.

1. Multiplying by One-Digit Numbers

Example 1. $4 \times 2 = 8$

ABCDEF	
. .	
2 0 0 4 0 0	Step 1
8	Step 2
2 0 0 0 0 8	Result

A B C D E F	A B C D E F
Fig. 86	Fig. 87

Step 1: Set the multiplicand 4 on the unit rod D and the multiplier 2 on rod A, thus leaving two vacant rods between the numbers as in Fig. 86

Step 2 : Multiply the multiplicand 4 by the multiplier 2. Set the product 8 on F, the second rod to the right of the multiplicand, and clear rod D of its 4. Fig. 87 shows the result of Step 2.

Note : The accompanying diagram shows another way to illustrate the same problem. Here the two figures in the row designated Step 1 indicate that the multiplier 2 and the multiplicand 4 have been set on A and D respectively. The two figures in the row designated Result show the multiplier 2 remaining on A and the product 8 which has been set on F as the result of the multiplication.

All the following examples will be illustrated in the two ways shown above.

The reasons for clearing off the multiplicand after its multiplication will be given at the end the section on multiplication by two-digit numbers.

Example 2. $8 \times 6 = 48$

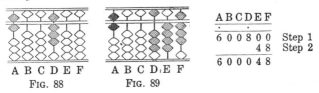

A	B	C	D	E	F	
.			.			
6	0	0	8	0	0	Step 1
				4	8	Step 2
6	0	0	0	4	8	

A B C D E F
Fig. 88

A B C D₁E F
Fig. 89

Step 1 : Set 8 on the unit rod D and 6 on A, leaving two vacant rods (Fig. 88).

Step 2 : Multiplying 8 by 6, set the product 48 on EF, and clear D of its 8. In this step, the first rod to the right of the multiplicand, designated E, is the tens' rod of the product 48 (Fig. 89).

Note : Some experts say it is desirable to clear away the multiplicand before setting the product. For instance, in the above example, they say that the product 48 should be set on

EF after clearing D of its 8. This method has the merit of saving the time of shifting the hand back to the left to clear off the multiplicand after setting the product. But the Abacus Committee frowns upon this procedure, saying that, especially for beginners, it is apt to cause confusion in that the multiplicand must be carried in the memory after it has been cleared away from the board.

Example 3. $24 \times 7 = 168$

	A	B	C	D	E	F	G	
A B C D E F G								
7	0	0	2	4	0	0		Step 1
						2	8	Step 2
7	0	0	2	0	2	8		
					1	4		Step 3
7	0	0	0	1	6	8		

Step 1: Set 24 on DE, with E as the unit rod, and set 7 on A (Fig. 90).

Step 2: Multiplying the 4 in 24 by 7, set the product 28 on FG, and clear E of its 4 (Fig. 91).

Step 3: Multiplying the remaining 2 in 24 by 7, set the product 14 on EF, thereby adding this new product to the 28 on FG, and clear E of its 2. This makes a total of 168 on EFG, which is the answer (Fig. 92).

Note 1: The reason for setting the product 14 on the rods EF, which are one place higher than FG, is obvious. When adding 14, do not take the trouble of thinking that this product is 140 in actual value and that therefore this must be set on EF. Instead just mechanically set the 1 in 14 on E and add the 4 in 14 to the previous 2 on F, and let the result form itself automatically.

Note 2: In Step 2, F is the tens' rod of the product 28, while in Step 3, E is the tens' rod of the product 14. In each step of multiplication, the first rod to the right of that figure in the multiplicand which is multiplied is the tens' rod of the product.

Note 3 : When there are two digits in the multiplicand, first multiply the last digit by the multiplier and then the first digit.

2. Multiplying by Two-Digit Numbers

Example 4. $8 \times 17 = 136$

A B C D E F G H	A B C D E F G H	A B C D E F G H
FIG. 93	FIG. 94	FIG. 95

```
A B C D E F G H
    .       .
1 7 0 0 8 0 0 0   Step 1
            8     Step 2
        + 5 6     Step 3
1 7 0 0 0 1 3 6
```

Step 1 : Set 8 on the unit rod **E** and 17 on AB (Fig. 93).

Step 2 : Multiplying the 8 by the 1 in 17, set the product 8 on G (Fig. 94).

Step 3 : Multiplying the 8 by the 7 in 17, set the product 56 on GH, and clear E of its 8. Since you already have 8 on G, you get, on FGH, a total of 136, which is the answer (Fig. 95).

Note : When there are two digits in the multiplier, first multiply the multiplicand by the first digit of the multiplier and next by the last digit of the multiplier.

Example 5. $46 \times 23 = 1,058$

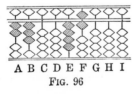

A B C D E F G H I	A B C D E F G H I
FIG. 96	FIG. 97

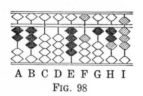

A B C D E F G H I		
· · ·		
2 3 0 0 4 6 0 0 0		Step 1
1 2		Step 2
+ 1 8		Step 3
2 3 0 0 4 0 1 3 8		
+ 8		Step 4
+ 1 2		Step 5
2 3 0 0 0 1 0 5 8		

Fig. 98

Step 1 : Set 46 on EF, with F as the unit rod, and set 23 on AB (Fig. 96).

Step 2 : Multiplying the 6 in 46 by the 2 in 23, set the product 12 on GH (Fig. 97).

Step 3 : Multiplying the same 6 in 46 by the 3 in 23, set the product 18 on HI and clear F of its 6. Since you have 12 on GH, you get a total of 138 on GHI (Fig. 98). Remember that each time the same digit in the multiplicand is multiplied by one digit after another in the multiplier, the value of the product is reduced by one rod or place.

A B C D E F G H I

Fig. 99

Fig. 100

Step 4 : Multiplying the 4 in 46 by the 2 in 23, set the product 8 on G. This makes a total of 938 on GHI (Fig. 99).

Step 5 : Multiplying the same 4 in 46 by the 3 in 23, set the product 12 on GH and clear E of its 4. This leaves the answer 1,058 on FGHI (Fig. 100).

Note : In case both the multiplier and the multiplicand have two digits, (1) multiply the last digit of the multiplicand by the first digit of the multiplier; (2) multiply the same digit of the multiplicand by the last digit of the multiplier; (3) multiply the first digit of the multiplicand by the first digit of the multiplier; and (4) multiply the same first digit of the multiplicand by the last digit of the multiplier. This is the fundamental rule of multiplication.

Example 6. $97 \times 48 = 4,656$

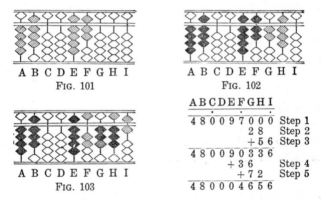

	A B	C D	E F	G H	I	
Fig. 101						

	A B	C D	E F	G H	I	
Fig. 102						

A B C D E F G H I

4 8 0 0 9 7 0 0 0	Step 1
2 8	Step 2
+ 5 6	Step 3
4 8 0 0 9 0 3 3 6	
+ 3 6	Step 4
+ 7 2	Step 5
4 8 0 0 0 4 6 5 6	

A B C D E F G H I

Fig. 103

Step 1: Set 97 on EF, with F as the unit rod, and set 48 on AB (Fig. 101).

Step 2: Multiplying the 7 in 97 by the 4 in 48, set the product 28 on GH (Fig. 102).

Step 3: Multiplying the same 7 in 97 by the 8 in 48, set the product 56 on HI, and clear F of its 7. Since you have 28 on GH, you get a total of 336 on GHI (Fig. 103).

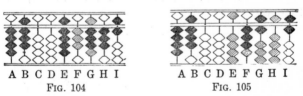

A B C D E F G H I

Fig. 104

A B C D E F G H I

Fig. 105

Step 4: Multiplying the remaining 9 in 97 by the 4 in 48, set the product 36 on FG. This makes a total of 3,936 on

FGHI (Fig. 104).

Step 5: Multiplying the same 9 in 97 by the 8 in 48, set the product 72 on GH, and clear E of its 9. This gives you, on FGHI, a total of 4,656, which is the answer (Fig. 105).

Note: The preceding examples will have indicated the desirability of clearing off each digit in the multiplicand after its multiplication by all the digits in the multiplier. If you did not do so, you would be greatly inconvenienced in operation. This is especially the case when the multiplicand is a large number. First, you would often find it hard to tell which of the digits in the multiplicand you had multiplied by all the digits in the multiplier. Second, this incorrect procedure would necessitate the removal of the multiplier further to the right beyond the product of the correct procedure by as many digits as there are in the multiplicand.

3. Multiplying by Numbers of Over Two-Digits

No matter how many digits the multiplier may have, the principle of multiplication is the same as that of multiplying by two-digit numbers. You have only to see that you do not mistake the order of multiplication and the rods on which to to set products.

Example 7. $37 \times 432 = 15,984$

Step 1: Set 37 on FG, with G as the unit rod, and set 432 on ABC (Fig. 106).

Step 2: Multiplying the 7 in 37 by the 4 in 432, set the

A B C D E F G H I J K
FIG. 106

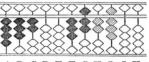

A B C D E F G H I J K
FIG. 107

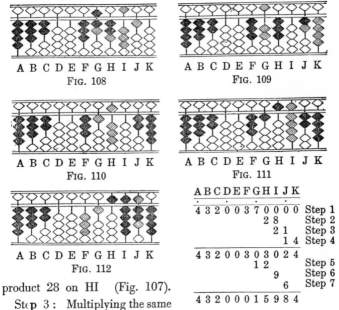

A B C D E F G H I J K
FIG. 108

A B C D E F G H I J K
FIG. 109

A B C D E F G H I J K
FIG. 110

A B C D E F G H I J K
FIG. 111

A B C D E F G H I J K
FIG. 112

A B C D E F G H I J K	
4 3 2 0 0 3 7 0 0 0 0	Step 1
2 8	Step 2
2 1	Step 3
1 4	Step 4
4 3 2 0 0 3 0 3 0 2 4	
1 2	Step 5
9	Step 6
6	Step 7
4 3 2 0 0 0 1 5 9 8 4	

product 28 on HI   (Fig. 107).

Step 3 : Multiplying the same
7 in 37 by the 3 in 432, set the product 21 on IJ.   This
makes a total of 301 on HIJ (Fig. 108).

Step 4 : Multiplying the same 7 in 37 by the 2 in 432,
set the product 14 on JK, and clear G of its 7. This makes
a total of 3,024 on HIJK   (Fig. 109).

Step 5 : Multiplying the 3 in 37 by the 4 in 432, set the
product 12 on GH. This makes a total of 15,024 on GHIJK
(Fig. 110).

Step 6 : Multiplying the 3 in 37 by the 3 in 432, set the
product 9 on I. This makes a total of 15,924 on GHIJK
(Fig. 111).

Step 7 : Multiplying the 3 in 37 by the 2 in 432, set the
product 6 on J, and clear F of its 3. This makes, on GHIJK,

a total of 15,984, which is the answer   (Fig. 112).

Example 8. $78 \times 503 = 39,234$

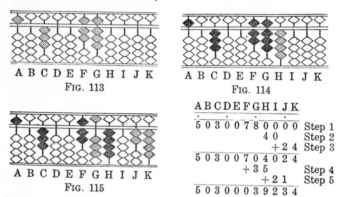

ABCDEFGHIJK		
FIG. 113		

FIG. 114

ABCDEFGHIJK		
5 0 3 0 0 7 8 0 0 0 0		Step 1
4 0		Step 2
+ 2 4		Step 3
5 0 3 0 0 7 0 4 0 2 4		
+ 3 5		Step 4
+ 2 1		Step 5
5 0 3 0 0 0 3 9 2 3 4		

A B C D E F G H I J K
FIG. 115

Step 1: Set 78 on FG, with G as the unit rod, and set 503 on ABC (Fig. 113).

Step 2: Multiplying the 8 in 78 by the 5 in 508, set the 4 of the product 40 on H (Fig. 114).

Step 3: Multiplying the same 8 in 78 by the 3 in 503, set the product 24 on JK and clear G of the 8. This makes a total of 4,024 on HIJK. In setting this product skip rod I as the second figure of the multiplier 503 is zero. In other words, the product must be set on JK instead of on IJ (Fig. 115).

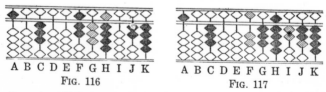

A B C D E F G H I J K
FIG. 116

A B C D E F G H I J K
FIG. 117

Step 4: Multiplying the 7 in 78 by the 5 in 503, set the product 35 on GH. This makes a total of 39,024 on GHIJK

(Fig. 116).

Step 5: Multiplying the same 7 in 78 by the 3 in 503, set the product 21 on IJ instead of HI, as the second figure of 503 is zero, and clear F of its 7. This leaves, on GHIJK, a total of 39,234, which is the answer (Fig. 117).

4. Exercises

Group I

1. $34 \times 4 = 136$
2. $23 \times 5 = 115$
3. $12 \times 4 = 48$
4. $32 \times 3 = 96$
5. $21 \times 5 = 105$
6. $33 \times 45 = 1,485$
7. $52 \times 56 = 2,912$
8. $23 \times 65 = 1,495$
9. $53 \times 75 = 3,975$
10. $25 \times 85 = 2,125$

11. $21 \times 23 = 483$
12. $12 \times 32 = 384$
13. $21 \times 43 = 903$
14. $12 \times 56 = 672$
15. $31 \times 64 = 1,984$
16. $43 \times 56 = 2,408$
17. $32 \times 64 = 2,048$
18. $53 \times 76 = 4,028$
19. $23 \times 83 = 1,909$
20. $35 \times 96 = 3,360$

Group II

1. $112 \times 23 = 2,576$
2. $123 \times 35 = 4,305$
3. $212 \times 46 = 9,752$
4. $345 \times 57 = 19,665$
5. $423 \times 64 = 27,072$
6. $513 \times 76 = 38,988$
7. $607 \times 87 = 52,809$
8. $452 \times 85 = 38,420$
9. $631 \times 95 = 59,945$
10. $608 \times 97 = 58,976$

11. $1,023 \times 34 = 34,782$
12. $3,243 \times 45 = 145,935$
13. $4,352 \times 58 = 252,416$
14. $5,624 \times 67 = 376,808$
15. $6,712 \times 78 = 523,536$
16. $132 \times 334 = 44,088$
17. $234 \times 456 = 106,704$
18. $431 \times 467 = 201,277$
19. $546 \times 686 = 374,556$
20. $756 \times 879 = 664,524$

VI. DIVISION

There are two fundamental methods of division on the abacus. The older method, though still favored by some, has fallen out of general use since about 1930 because it requires the memorization of a special division table. The newer method, which is the easier to learn because it uses the multiplication instead of the division table, is the standard one now taught in grade schools, and will be introduced in the following pages. Strictly speaking, it is not new, as it has long been used, but only in a very limited use until around 1930 when it was improved and publicized. Standard terminology will be used in describing the method. For example, in the problem $50 \div 5 = 10$, 50 is the dividend, 5 the divisor, and 10 the quotient.

It is customary to set the dividend a little to the right of the central part of the abacus and the divisor at the left. The two numbers are generally separated by three or four unused rods. As the Abacus Committee favors leaving four unused rods between the two numbers, the following examples will adhere to that practice.

The method of division used here gives the first digit of the quotient between the dividend and divisor. Two main reasons can be given for setting the dividend on the right and the divisor on the left. One is that since the abacus is operated with the right hand, the reverse order of setting the two numbers would cause the multiplier to be hidden by the hand much of the time, as in the case of multiplication. The other is that in case the dividend is indivisible by the divisor, the reverse order would cause the quotient to extend right into the divisor.

In division, as in multiplication, the use of the unit rod is not too essential, but does facilitate calculation in many ways. Therefore, the unit figure of the dividend is always set on a unit rod. When the divisor is a whole number, however, we shall disregard the unit rod, and simply set the divisor in such a way that its last digit is located on the fifth rod to the left of the dividend.

As for the order of setting the dividend and divisor, since the last digit of the dividend must be set on a unit rod, it is advisable for the beginner to set the dividend before setting the divisor. As is the case with multiplication, however, experts often reverse the procedure, setting the divisor first or not at all.

1. Dividing by One-Digit Numbers

Example 1. $8 \div 2 = 4$

A B C D E F
FIG. 118

A B C D E F
FIG. 119

A B C D E F	
2 0 0 0 0 8	Step 1
4	Step 2
− 8	
2 0 0 4 0 0	Result

Step 1 : Set the dividend 8 on rod F and the divisor 2 on rod A, with four vacant rods between the two numbers. Make sure that F is a unit rod marked with a unit point (Fig. 118).

Step 2 : Mentally divide 8 by 2 ($8 \div 2 = 4$); set the quotient 4 on D, the second rod to the left of the dividend; and clear

F of its 8. Fig. 119 and the row of figures designated Result in the diagram show the result of this step.

Example 2 $837 \div 3 = 279$

A B C D E F G H
FIG. 120

A B C D E F G H
FIG. 121

```
A B C D E F G H
  .     .     .
3 0 0 0 0 8 3 7   Step 1
        2         Step 2
      – 6
3 0 0 2 0 2 3 7
        7         Step 3
      – 2 1
3 0 0 2 7 0 2 7
        9         Step 4
      – 2 7
3 0 0 2 7 9 0 0
```

Step 1: Set 837 on the rods FGH, with H as the unit rod, and set 3 on A (Fig. 120).

Step 2: Compare the 3 with the 8 in 837. 3 goes into 8 twice with 2 left over. Set the quotient figure 2 on D, the second rod to the left of 8 in 837. Next multiply the divisor 3 by this quotient figure 2, and subtract the product 6 from the 8 on F. This leaves 2 on F (Fig. 121).

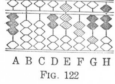

A B C D E F G H
FIG. 122

A B C D E F G H
FIG. 123

Step 3: Compare the 3 with 23 on FG. The 2 on F is the remainder left over as a result of the previous step. 3 goes into 23 seven times with 2 left over. Set 7 as the quotient figure on E. Next multiply the divisor 3 by this 7, and subtract the product 21 from the 23 on FG. This leaves 2 on G (Fig. 122).

Step 4: Compare the 3 with 27 on GH. The 2 on G is the

remainder left over as a result of the second step. 3 goes into 27 nine times. Set the quotient figure 9 on F. Next multiply the 3 by this 9, and subtract the product 27 from the 27 on GH. This clears GH and leaves the answer 279 on DEF (Fig. 123).

Note: Answers to problems in division can be easily checked by multiplication. Thus, to check the foregoing answer, simply multiply the quotient 279 on DEF by the divisor 3, that is, the number you originally divided by, and you will get the product 837 on FGH, i. e., the same rods on which you had 837 as the dividend. By this checking the student will see that the position of the quotient in division is that of the multiplicand in multiplication, and that the position of the dividend in division is that of the product in multiplication. Therefore, we may say that the methods of multiplication and division introduced in this book form the counterpart of each other.

Example 3.　　6,013 ÷ 7 = 859

A B C D E F G H I
FIG. 124

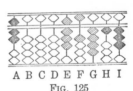

A B C D E F G H I
FIG. 125

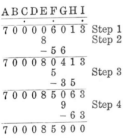

ABCDEFGHI

7	0	0	0	0	6	0	1	3	Step 1
	8								Step 2
				− 5	6				
7	0	0	0	8	0	4	1	3	
				5					Step 3
				− 3	5				
7	0	0	0	8	5	0	6	3	
					9				Step 4
					− 6	3			
7	0	0	0	8	5	9	0	0	

Step 1: Set 6,013 on FGHI, with I as the unit rod, and set 7 on A (Fig. 124).

Step 2: Compare the divisor 7 with the 6 in 6,013. 7 will not go into 6. So compare the 7 with the 60 in 6,013. 7 goes into 60 eight times. In this case set the quotient figure 8 on E, the first rod to the left of the first digit of the

dividend. Next multiply the divisor 7 by this 8, and subtract
the product 56 from the 60 on FG. This leaves 4 on G
(Fig. 125).

A B C D E F G H I

FIG. 126

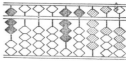

A B C D E F G H I

FIG. 127

Step 3 : Compare the 7 with 41 on GH. 7 goes into 41
five times. Set the quotient figure 5 on F. Next multiply the
7 by this 5, and subtract the product 35 from the 41 on GH.
This leaves 6 on H (Fig. 126).

Step 4 : Compare the 7 with 63 remaining on HI. 7 goes
into 63 nine times. Set the quotient figure 9 on G. Next
multiply the 7 by this 9, and subtract the product 63 from
the 63 remaining on HI. This clears HI, and leaves the answer
859 on EFG (Fig. 127).

Note : When the divisor is larger than the first digit of the
dividend, compare it with the first two digits of the dividend.
In this case set the quotient figure on the first rod to the left
of the first digit of the dividend. The chief merit of this procedure is that, in checking, the quotient multiplied by the divisor gives the product on the very rods on which the dividend
was located previous to its division.

This procedure is the same as the principle of graphic division. In dividing 36 by 2, you write the quotient figure 1
above the 3 in 36. But in dividing 36 by 4, you write the
quotient figure 9 above the 6 in 36. On the abacus board the
quotient figure cannot be put above the dividend. So in dividing 36 by 2, the first quotient figure 1 is set on the second
rod to the left of 36, while in dividing 36 by 4, the quotient

figure 9 is set on the first rod to the left of 36.

2. Dividing by Two-Digit Numbers

Example 4. $552 \div 23 = 24$

A B C D E F G H I
Fig. 128

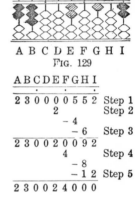

A B C D E F G H I
Fig. 129

A B C D E F G H I	
. . .	
2 3 0 0 0 0 5 5 2	Step 1
2	Step 2
– 4	
– 6	Step 3
2 3 0 0 2 0 0 9 2	
4	Step 4
– 8	
– 1 2	Step 5
2 3 0 0 2 4 0 0 0	

A B C D E F G H I
Fig. 130

Step 1: Set 552 on GHI, with I as the unit rod, and set 23 on AB (Fig. 128).

Step 2: Compare the 2 in 23 with the 5 in 552. 2 goes into 5 two times. Set the quotient figure 2 on E, the second rod to the left of the 5 in 552. Next multiply the 2 in 23 by this quotient figure 2, and subtract the product 4 from the 5 on G. This leaves 1 on G (Fig. 129).

Step 3: Now multiply the 3 in 23 by the same quotient figure 2, and subtract the product 6 from 15 on GH. This leaves 9 on H (Fig. 130).

A B C D E F G H I
Fig. 131

A B C D E F G H I
Fig. 132

Step 4: Compare the 2 in 23 with the 9 on H. 2 goes into 9 four times. Set the quotient figure 4 on F. Next multiply the 2 in 23 by this quotient figure 4, and subtract the product 8 from the 9 on H. This leaves 1 on H (Fig. 131).

Step 5: Multiply the 3 in 23 by the same 4, and subtract the product 12 from the 12 remaining on HI. This clears HI and leaves the answer 24 on EF (Fig. 132).

Example 5. $6,308 \div 83 = 76$

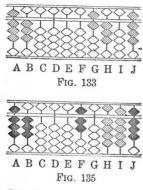

A B C D E F G H I J
FIG. 133

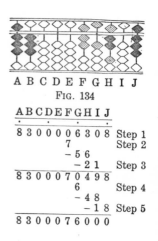

A B C D E F G H I J
FIG. 134

A	B	C	D	E	F	G	H	I	J	
·				·			·		·	
8	3	0	0	0	0	6	3	0	8	Step 1
						7				Step 2
					−	5	6			
						−	2	1		Step 3
8	3	0	0	0	7	0	4	9	8	
						6				Step 4
					−	4	8			
						−	1	8		Step 5
8	3	0	0	0	7	6	0	0	0	

A B C D E F G H I J
FIG. 135

Step 1: Set 6,308 on GHIJ, with J as the unit rod, and set 83 on AB (Fig. 133).

Step 2: Compare the 8 in 83 with the 6 in 6,308. 8 will not go into 6. So compare the 8 with the 63 in 6,308. 8 goes into 63 seven times. Set the quotient figure 7 on F, the first rod to the left of the 6 in 6,308. Next multiply the 8 in 83 by this 7 in the quotient, and subtract the product 56 from the 63 on GH. This leaves 7 on H (Fig. 134).

Step 3: Multiply the 3 in 83 by the same quotient figure 7, and subtract the product 21 from 70 on HI. This leaves 49 on HI (Fig. 135).

A B C D E F G H I J
Fig. 136

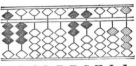

A B C D E F G H I J
Fig. 137

Step 4: Compare the 8 in 83 with the 49 on HI. 8 goes into 49 six times. Set the quotient figure 6 on G. Next multiply the 8 in 83 by this 6, and subtract the product 48 from the 49 on HI. This leaves 1 on I (Fig. 136).

Step 5: Multiply the 3 in 83 by the same quotient figure 6, and subtract the product 18 from 18 on IJ. This clears IJ and leaves the answer 76 on FG (Fig. 137).

Note: In case the divisor is a two-digit number, do not take the trouble of comparing its two digits with the first two or three digits of the dividend to work out the correct quotient figure mentally. Simply compare the first digit of the divisor with that of the dividend. When the first digit of the divisor is larger than that of the dividend, compare it with the first two digits of the dividend. In case quotient figures tried are incorrect, correct them by the methods shown in Examples 6, 7, and 8 instead of perplexing yourself with mental arithmetic. Thus make the most of the chief advantage of the abacus, the complete mechanical process which minimizes mental labor, and experience will enable you to find correct quotient figures at a glance.

Example 6. $4,698 \div 54 = 87$

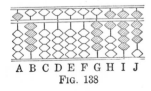

A B C D E F G H I J
Fig. 138

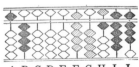

A B C D E F G H I J
Fig. 139

This example shows how the process of division must be revised when too large a quotient figure has been used.

```
A B C D E F G H I J
·       ·       ·   ·
5 4 0 0 0 0 4 6 9 8   Step 1
            9         Step 2
          - 4 5
          -(3 6)
5 4 0 0 0 9 0 1 9 8
            - 1       Step 3 (revision)
            + 5
5 4 0 0 0 8 0 6 9 8
          - 3 2       Step 4 (revision)
5 4 0 0 0 8 0 3 7 8
            7         Step 5
          - 3 5
          - 2 8       Step 6
5 4 0 0 0 8 7 0 0 0
```

Step 1: Set 4,698 on GHIJ, with J as the unit rod, and set 54 on AB (Fig. 138).

Step 2: The 5 in 54 will not go into the 4 in 4,698. So compare the 5 with the 46 in 4,698. 5 goes into 46 nine times. Now suppose you have tried 9 as the quotient figure instead of the correct 8 and have set it on F. Then you will multiply the 5 in 54 by 9, and subtract the product 45 from the 46 on GH. This leaves 1 on H. Next multiplying the 4 in 54 by the same 9, you will find that the product 36 is larger than the 19 remaining on HI and that you ought to have tried a quotient figure one less than 9 (Fig. 139).

A B C D E F G H I J
FIG. 140

A B C D E F G H I J
FIG. 141

Step 3: To revise the incorrect quotient figure 9 to 8, subtract 1 from the 9 on F, and you get the new quotient figure 8 on F. Next multiply the 5 in 54 by 1, i. e., the difference between the quotient figures 9 and 8, and add the product 5 to the 1 on H. Now you have 6 on H (Fig. 140).

Step 4: Multiply the 4 in 54 by the new quotient figure 8, and subtract the product 32 from 69 on HI. This leaves

37 on HI (Fig. 141).

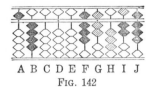

A B C D E F G H I J
Fig. 142

A B C D E F G H I J
Fig. 143

Step 5: Compare the 5 in 54 with the 37 on HI. 5 goes into 37 seven times. So set the quotient figure 7 on G. Next multiply the 5 in 54 by this 7, and subtract the product 35 from the 37 on HI. This leaves 2 on I (Fig. 142).

Step 6: Multiply the 4 in 54 by the same quotient figure 7, and subtract the product 28 from 28 remaining on IJ. This clears IJ and leaves the answer 87 on FG (Fig. 143).

Example 7. $1,666 \div 17 = 98$

This example shows how a problem of division is worked when the first digit of both divisor and dividend are the same.

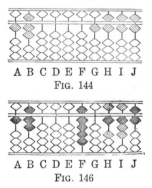

A B C D E F G H I J
Fig. 144

Fig. 146

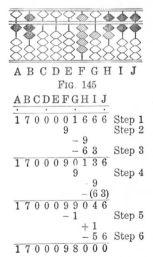

A B C D E F G H I J
Fig. 145

A B C D E F G H I J	
. . . .	
1 7 0 0 0 0 1 6 6 6	Step 1
9	Step 2
− 9	
− 6 3	Step 3
1 7 0 0 0 9 0 1 3 6	
9	Step 4
9	
−(6 3)	
1 7 0 0 0 9 9 0 4 6	
− 1	Step 5
+ 1	
− 5 6	Step 6
1 7 0 0 0 9 8 0 0 0	

Step 1: Set 1,666 on GHIJ, with J as the unit rod, and set 17 on AB (Fig. 144).

Step 2: When the first digit of the divisor and the dividend are the same, as in this example, compare the second digits of the two numbers. In such a situation, if the second digit of the dividend is smaller than that of the divisor, try 9 as the quotient figure. If 9 is too large, try 8 as in Step 5 of this example. If 8 is still too large, go on trying a quotient figure one less till the correct one is found. In such a case 9 is the figure likeliest to be correct.

Now try 9 as the quotient figure and set it on F, the first rod to the left of the first digit of the dividend. Next multiply the 1 in 17 by this 9 and subtract the product 9 from 16 on GH. This leaves 7 on H (Fig. 145).

Step 3: Multiply the 7 in 17 by this same 9, and subtract the product 63 from 76 on HI. This leaves 13 on HI (Fig. 146).

Step 4: The 1 in 17 and the 1 remaining on H are the same. So compare the 7 in 17 and the 3 remaining on I. 3 is smaller than 7. So

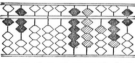

A B C D E F G H I J
FIG. 147

try 9 as the quotient figure and set it on G. Now multiply the 1 in 17 by this 9 and subtract the product 9 from the 13 on HI. This leaves 4 on I. Next, multiplying the 7 in 17 by this same 9, you will see that the product 63 is larger than 46 remaining on IJ. So you will find that you ought to have tried 8 as the quotient figure (Fig. 147).

A B C D E F G H I J
FIG. 148

A B C D E F G H I J
FIG. 149

Step 5: To revise the incorrect quotient figure 9 to 8, subtract 1 from the 9 on G. Next you must revise the division in Step 4. So multiply the 1 in 17 by 1, the difference between the 9 and 8, and add the product 1 to the 4 remaining on I. Then you get 5 on I (Fig. 148).

Step 6: Multiply the 7 in 17 by the new quotient figure 8 and subtract the product 56 from 56 on IJ. This clears IJ and leaves the answer 98 on FG (Fig. 149).

Note: In cases where the first digits of both the divisor and the dividend are the same, if the second digit of the dividend is larger than that of the divisor, set 1 as the quotient figure on the second rod to the left of the first digit of the dividend. An instance is given in Example 9.

Example 8.   7,644÷84=91

This example is to show how division is to be revised when the quotient figure tried is too small.

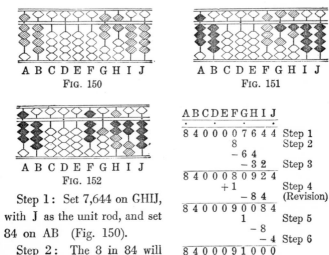

A B C D E F G H I J
FIG. 150

A B C D E F G H I J
FIG. 151

A B C D E F G H I J
FIG. 152

Step 1: Set 7,644 on GHIJ, with J as the unit rod, and set 84 on AB (Fig. 150).

Step 2: The 8 in 84 will

A B C D E F G H I J	
8 4 0 0 0 0 7 6 4 4	Step 1
8	Step 2
− 6 4	
− 3 2	Step 3
8 4 0 0 0 8 0 9 2 4	
+ 1	Step 4
− 8 4	(Revision)
8 4 0 0 0 9 0 0 8 4	
1	Step 5
− 8	
− 4	Step 6
8 4 0 0 0 9 1 0 0 0	

not go into the 7 in 7,644. So compare the 8 with the 76 in 7,644. 8 goes into 76 nine times. So you ought to try 9 as the quotient figure. But suppose by mistake you have tried 8 as the quotient figure instead of the correct 9 and have set it on F. Then you will multiply the 8 in 84 by 8 and subtract the product 64 from the 76 on GH. This will leave 12 on GH (Fig. 151).

Step 3: Multiplying the 4 in 84 by the same quotient figure 8, you will subtract the product 32 from 124 on GHI. Then you will find that the remainder 92 is larger than 84 and that you ought to have tried 9, i.e., a quotient figure one more than 8 (Fig. 152).

Step 4: To revise the incorrect quotient figure 8 to 9, add 1 to the quotient figure 8 on F. Next multiply the divisor 84 by 1, i. e., the difference between the two quotient figures, 8 and 9, and subtract the product 84 from the 92 on HI. This leaves 8 on I (Fig. 153).

A B C D E F G H I J
FIG. 153

A B C D E F G H I J
FIG. 154

Step 5: The 8 in 84 and the 8 remaining on I are the same. So compare the 4 in 84 with the 4 remaining on J, and you can see that they are also the same. Therefore, set the quotient figure 1 on G. Now, multiplying the 8 in 84 by 1, subtract the product 8 from the 8 on I. Next multiplying the 4 in 84 by the same 1, subtract the product 4 from the 4 on J. This clears IJ and leaves the quotient 91 on FG (Fig. 154).

3. Dividing by Numbers of Over Two-Digits

Example 9.   3,978÷234=17

A B C D E F G H I J K
FIG. 155

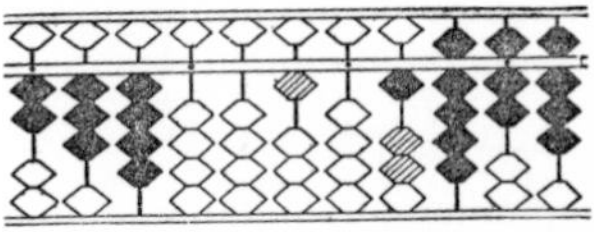

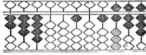

A B C D E F G H I J K
FIG. 157

Step 1: Set 3,978 on HIJK, with K as the unit rod, and set 234 on ABC (Fig. 155).

Step 2: Compare the 2 in 234 with the 3 in 3,978. 2 goes into 3 one time. Set the quotient figure 1 on F, the second rod to the left of the 3 in 3,978. Now multiply the 2 in 234 by this quotient figure 1, and subtract the product 2 from the 3 on H. This leaves 1 on H (Fig. 156).

A B C D E F G H I J K
FIG. 156

A B C D E F G H I J K
FIG. 158

```
A B C D E F G H I J K
      ·   · ·    ·   ·
2 3 4 0 0 0 0 3 9 7 8   Step 1
          1             Step 2
          - 2
            - 3         Step 3
              - 4       Step 4
2 3 4 0 0 1 0 1 6 3 8
          8             Step 5
          - 1 6
          -( 2 4)
2 3 4 0 0 1 8 0 0 3 8
          - 1           Step 6
          + 2
2 3 4 0 0 1 0 0 2 3 8
          7
            - 2 1       Step 7
            - 2 8       Step 8
2 3 4 0 0 1 7 0 0 0 0
```

Step 3: Multiply the 3 in 234 by the same quotient figure 1, and subtract the product 3 from 9 on I. This leaves 6 on I and 167 on HIJ (Fig. 157).

Step 4: Multiply the 4 in 234 by the same quotient figure 1, and subtract the product 4 from 7 on J. This leaves 3 on

J and 1,638 on HIJK   (Fig. 158).

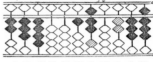

A B C D E F G H I J K

FIG. 159

A B C D E F G H I J K

FIG. 160

Step 5 :   Compare the 2 in 234 with the 16 remaining on HI.   2 goes into 16 eight times.   Suppose you have tried 8 as the quotient figure instead of the correct 7 and have set it on G.   Then you will multiply the 2 in 234 by 8, and subtract the product 16 from the 16 on HI.   This clears HI.   Next, multiplying the 3 in 234 by the same 8, you will find that the product 24 is larger than 3 remaining on J, and that you ought to have tried a quotient figure one less than 8   (Fig. 159).

Step 6 :   To revise the incorrect quotient figure 8 to 7, subtract 1 from the 8 on G, and you get the new quotient figure 7 on G.   Next multiply the 2 in 234 by 1, i. e., the difference between the quotient figures 8 and 7, and set the product 2 on I.   Now you have 2 on I and 234 on IJK   (Fig. 160).

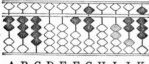

A B C D E F G H I J K

FIG. 161

A B C D E F G H I J K

FIG. 162

Step 7 :   Multiply the 3 in 234 by the new quotient figure 7, and subtract the product 21 from 23 on IJ.   This leaves 2 on J and 28 on JK   (Fig. 161).

Step 8 :   Next multiply the 4 in 234 by the same new quotient figure 7, and subtract the product 28 from 28 on JK. This clears JK and leaves the answer 17 on FG   (Fig. 162).

Example 10.   7,061 ÷ 307 = 23

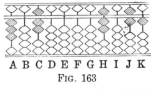

A B C D E F G H I J K

FIG. 163

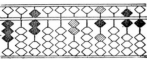

A B C D E F G H I J K

FIG. 164

```
A B C D E F G H I J K
  •        •     •     •
3 0 7 0 0 0 0 7 0 6 1   Step 1
          2             Step 2
        − 6
        − 1 4           Step 3
3 0 7 0 0 2 0 0 9 2 1
        3               Step 4
      − 9
      − 2 1             Step 5
3 0 7 0 0 2 3 0 0 0 0
```

A B C D E F G H I J K

FIG. 165

Step 1 : Set 7,061 on HIJK, with K as the unit rod, and set 307 on ABC, leaving as always four vacant rods between the two numbers (Fig. 163).

Step 2 : Comparing the 3 in 307 and the 7 in 7,061 you can see that 3 goes into 7 two times. Set the quotient figure 2 on F. Next multiply the 3 in 307 by this 2, and subtract the product 6 from the 7 on H. This leaves 1 on H (Fig. 164).

Step 3 : Multiply the 7 in 307 by the same quotient figure 2, and setting the product 14 on IJ, subtract it from 106 on HIJ. This leaves 92 on IJ. Since the second digit in 307 is zero, see that you set the product 14 on IJ instead of HI (Fig. 165).

A B C D E F G H I J K

FIG. 166

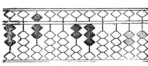

A B C D E F G H I J K

FIG. 167

Step 4 : The 3 in 307 goes into the 9 on I three times.

So set the quotient figure 3 on G. Next multiply the 3 in 307 by this quotient figure 3 and subtract the product 9 from the 9 on I. This leaves 21 on JK (Fig. 166).

Step 5: Multiply the 7 in 307 by the same quotient figure 3 and subtract the product 21 from the 21 on JK. This clears JK and leaves the answer 23 on FG (Fig. 167).

4. Key to Finding Correct Quotient Figures

1. When the first digit in the divisor is 5, twice the first digit in the dividend often proves a correct quotient figure.

2. When the first digit in the divisor is 9, the first digit in the dividend often proves a correct quotient figure.

3. When the first digit in the divisor is larger than the second, it is safe to try a small quotient figure.

4. When the first digit in the divisor is smaller than the second, it is safe to try a large quotient figure.

5. Exercises

Group I

1.	$24 \div 2 = 12$	6.	$132 \div 12 = 11$
2	$36 \div 3 = 12$	7.	$441 \div 21 = 21$
3	$115 \div 5 = 23$	8.	$1,495 \div 65 = 23$
4.	$204 \div 6 = 34$	9.	$2,451 \div 57 = 43$
5.	$357 \div 7 = 51$	10.	$4,293 \div 81 = 53$

Group II

1.	$8,296 \div 68 = 122$	6.	$6,342 \div 453 = 14$
2	$4,270 \div 14 = 305$	7.	$9,728 \div 304 = 32$
3	$11,100 \div 75 = 148$	8.	$38,920 \div 695 = 56$
4	$7,560 \div 28 = 270$	9.	$46,113 \div 809 = 57$
5.	$24,957 \div 47 = 531$	10.	$26,460 \div 147 = 180$

VII. DECIMALS

In addition and subtraction the unit point serves as the mark of a decimal point, and the calculation of decimal problems is quite the same as that of whole numbers.

However, in multiplication and division, you cannot easily find the unit rod of the product and that of the quotient unless you know two rules covering the position of the decimal point of the product and two others covering the position of the decimal point of the quotient. These four rules may be best explained and illustrated in paired counterparts. The first pair of rules applies to whole or mixed-decimal numbers, and the second to decimal fractions.

Rule A. When the multiplier is a whole or a mixed decimal, the unit rod of the product moves to the right of that of the multiplicand by as many rods plus one as there are whole digits in the multiplier.

Rule B. When the divisor is a whole or a mixed decimal number, the unit rod of the quotient moves to the left of the unit rod of the dividend by as many rods plus one as there are whole digits in the divisor.

Rule C. When the multiplier is a decimal fraction whose first significant figure is in the tens place, the unit digit of the product is formed on the first rod to the right of the last digit of the multiplicand. Call this the basic rod. Then, each time the value of this multiplier is reduced by one place, the last digit of the product shifts by one rod to the left of this basic rod.

Rule D. When the divisor is a decimal fraction whose first significant figure is in the tens place, the unit digit of the quotient is formed on the first rod to the left of the last digit of the dividend. Call this the basic rod. Then, each time the value of this divisor is reduced by one place, the last digit of the quotient shifts by one rod to the right of this basic rod.

Example 1. (A) $4 \times 2 = 8$ (B) $8 \div 2 = 4$

```
                    ┌─────────── Unit rod of the multiplicand
                    │ ┌───────── Unit rod of the product
    (A)  A B C D E F                   (B)  A B C D E F
         •   •                              •   •
         2   4                              2       8
                 8                              4
                        Unit rod of the quotient ──────┐
                        Unit rod of the dividend ───────
```

As seen in the first diagram above, showing the position of the multiplier (Rod A), the multiplicand (Rod D), and the product (Rod F), when the multiplier is a one-digit number, the unit rod of the product moves by two rods to the right of that of the multiplicand. In other words, the last digit of the product is formed on the second rod to the right of that of the multiplicand.

As seen in the second diagram above, showing the position of the divisor (Rod A), the dividend (Rod F), and the quotient (Rod D), when the divisor is a one-digit number, the unit rod of the quotient moves by two rods to the left of that of the dividend. In other words, the last digit of the quotient is formed on the second rod to the left of that of the dividend.

Example 2. (A) $25 \times 15 = 375$ (B) $375 \div 15 = 25$

The first diagram below shows that when the multiplier is a two-digit number, the last digit of the product is formed on the third rod to the right of that of the multiplicand.

The second diagram below shows that when the divisor is a two-digit number, the last digit of the quotient is formed on the third rod to the left of that of the dividend.

```
                        .---------- Unit rod of the multiplicand
                        :    ....... Unit rod of the product
(A)  A B C D E F G H I          (B)  A B C D E F G H I
      ·     ·     ·                   ·     ·     ·
     1 5    2 5                       1 5          3 7 5
              3 7 5                        2 5
                               Unit rod of the quotient ------:
                               Unit rod of the dividend ------
```

Example 3. (A) $405 \times 123 = 49{,}815$ (B) $49{,}815 \div 123 = 405$

```
                        .---------- Unit rod of the multiplicand
                        :    .------ Unit rod of the product
(A)  A B C D E F G H I J K L    (A)  A B C D E F G H I J K L
      ·     ·     ·     ·             ·     ·     ·     ·
     1 2 3    4 0 5                   1 2 3          4 9 8 1 5
               4 9 8 1 5                   4 0 5
                               Unit rod of the quotient ------:
                               Unit rod of the dividend ------
```

The first diagram above shows that when the multiplier is a three-digit number, the last digit of the product is formed on the fourth rod to the right of that of the multiplicand.

The second diagram shows that when the divisor is a three-digit number, the last digit of the quotient is formed on the fourth rod to the left of that of the dividend.

Note on Example 3 (B): In case the dividend is separated from the divisor with four vacant rods, as in this example, the quotient product is clearly distinguishable from the divisor, since two vacant rods are left between them, thus : $\dfrac{\text{A B C D E F G H}}{1\ 2\ 3\ 0\ 0\ 4\ 0\ 5}$. But if the dividend were separated from the divisor with only three vacant rods, the quotient produced would be hardly distinguishable from the quotient, since only one vacant rod would be left between them thus : $\dfrac{\text{A B C D E F G}}{1\ 2\ 3\ 0\ 4\ 0\ 5}$. From this example the reader will see that in case the second figure of the quotient is a cipher, the quotient is hardly distinguishable from the divisor. Thus it is always preferable to set the divisor on the fifth instead of the fourth rod to the left of the dividend.

Example 4.   (A) $34 \times 1.2 = 40.8$ (B) $40.8 \div 1.2 = 34$

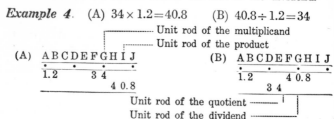

```
                          ┌─────────── Unit rod of the multiplicand
                          │  ┌──────── Unit rod of the product
 (A)   A B C D E F G H I J               (B)   A B C D E F G H I J
       •     •     •     •                     •     •     •     •
       ──────────────────                      ──────────────────
       1.2         3 4                          1.2         4 0.8
       ──────────────────                      ──────────────────
                     4 0.8                                  3 4
```

Unit rod of the quotient ─────── │ │
Unit rod of the dividend ───────────┘

Observe the first diagram above, and you will find that when the multiplier is a mixed number, the last whole digit of the product moves to the right of that of the multiplicand by as many rods plus one as there are whole digits in the multiplier.

Observe the second diagram, and you will find that when the divisor is a mixed number, the last whole digit of the quotient moves to the left of that of the dividend by as many rods plus one as there are whole digits in the divisor.

Example 5.   (C) $32 \times 0.4 = 12.8$ (C′) $98 \times 0.32 = 31.36$

               (D) $12.8 \div 0.4 = 32$ (D′) $31.36 \div 0.32 = 93$

```
                    ┌───────── Unit rod of the multiplicand ···┐
                    │  ┌────── Unit rod of the product ········┐│
 (C)   A B C D E F G H I             (C′)  A B C D E F G H I J
       •     •     •                       •     •     •     •
       ────────────────                    ──────────────────
       0.4         3 2                      0.3 2       9 8
       ────────────────                    ──────────────────
                     1 2.8                              3 1.3 6

 (D)   A B C D E F G H I             (D′)  A B C D E F G H I J K L
       •     •     •                       •     •     •     •
       ────────────────                    ────────────────────
       0.4       1 2.8                      0.3 2           3 1.3 6
       ────────────────                    ────────────────────
                 3 2                                        9 8
```

Unit rod of the dividend ─────────── │
Unit rod of the quotient ───────────┘

Diagrams C and C′ above show that when the divisor is a decimal fraction whose first significant figure is in the tenth place, the last whole digit of the product is formed on the first rod to the right of that of the multiplicand.

Diagrams D and D', above show that when the divisor is a decimal fraction whose first significant figure is in the tenth place, the last whole digit of the quotient is formed on the first rod to the left of that of the dividend.

Example 6.　(C)　$32 \times 0.04 = 1.28$　　(C')　$98 \times 0.032 = 3.136$
　　　　　　(D)　$1.28 \div 0.04 = 32$　　(D')　$3.136 \div 0.032 = 98$

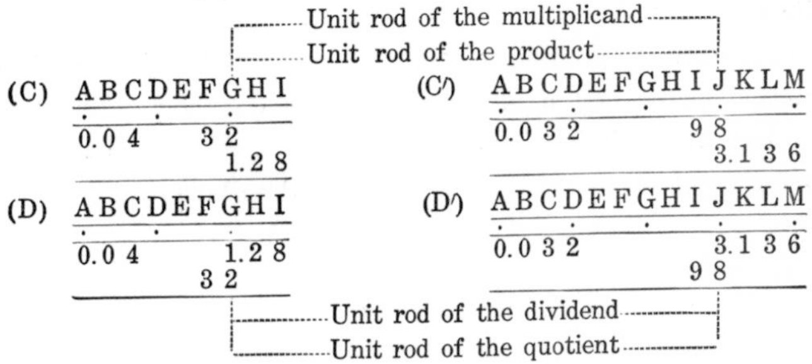

```
                �⌐ Unit rod of the multiplicand ············
                │ ┌········ Unit rod of the product ················┐
(C)  A B C D E F G H I           (C')  A B C D E F G H I J K L M
    ─────────────────                 ─────────────────────────────
      0. 0 4      3 2                    0. 0 3 2           9 8
                1. 2 8                                    3. 1 3 6

(D)  A B C D E F G H I           (D')  A B C D E F G H I J K L M
    ─────────────────                 ─────────────────────────────
      0. 0 4      1. 2 8                 0. 0 3 2         3. 1 3 6
                3 2                                        9 8
```

                           ┌·········· Unit rod of the dividend ··············┐
                           └·········· Unit rod of the quotient ···············

Diagrams C and C' above show that when the multiplier is a decimal fraction whose first significant figure is in the hundredth place, the last whole digit of the product is formed on the very rod on which that of the multiplicand is located.

Diagrams D and D' above show that when the divisor is a decimal fraction whose first significant figure is in the hundredth place, the last whole digit of the quotient is formed on the very rod on which that of the dividend is located.

Example 7.　(C)　$32 \times 0.004 = 0.128$　(C')　$98 \times 0.0032 = 0.3136$
　　　　　　(D)　$0.128 \div 0.004 = 32$　(D')　$0.3136 \div 0.0032 = 98$

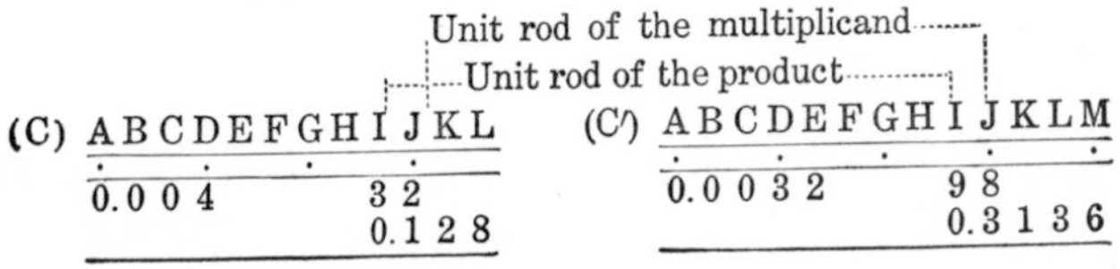

```
                  Unit rod of the multiplicand ·······
                  ┌···· Unit rod of the product ········┐
(C)  A B C D E F G H I J K L        (C')  A B C D E F G H I J K L M
    ─────────────────────               ─────────────────────────────
      0. 0 0 4      3 2                    0. 0 0 3 2          9 8
                  0. 1 2 8                                  0. 3 1 3 6
```

(D) A B C D E F G H I J K L M   (D') A B C D E F G H I J K L M N

0.0 0 4	0.1 2 8
	3 2

0.0 0 3 2	0.3 1 3 6
	9 8

⌐····Unit rod of the dividend········⌐
└····Unit rod of the quotient·········┘

Diagrams C and C' above show that when the multiplier is a decimal fraction whose first significant figure is in the thousandth place, the last whole digit of the product is formed on the first rod to the left of the last whole digit of the multiplicand.

Diagrams D and D' show that when the divisor is a decimal fraction whose first significant figure is in the thousandth place, the last whole digit of the quotient is formed on the first rod to the right of the last whole digit of the dividend.

VIII. MENTAL CALCULATION

All abacus experts can calculate mentally with miraculous rapidity. On an average they are twice as quick in mental calculation as on the abacus. It is possible for anyone to attain astonishing rapidity in such mental calculation by proper practice. The secret lies in applying abacus calculation to mental arithmetic by visualizing abacus manipulation.

Here are the vital points:

1. For example, in adding 24 to 76, close your eyes and visualize the beads of an abacus set to 76. Then mentally add 24 onto the beads, aiding your visualization of the abacus by flicking the index finger and thumb of your right hand as if really calculating on an abacus.

2. When adding a series of numbers, say, $24 + 76 + 62 + 50$, aid your memory by folding one of your left fingers each time the sum has come up to 100.

3. At first, practise the addition of numbers of two or more digits which come up to a round sum, for example, $76 + 24$, or $222 + 555 + 223$, and the like.

4. Remember, practising a few minutes at a time for many days is worth more than practising hours on a single day.

EXERCISES

Constant daily practice is essential if one is to become proficient in the use of the abacus. The following exercises, prepared and arranged in accordance with the most up-to-date methods, have been kindly furnished by Professor Miyokichi Ban, an outstanding abacus authority. They will provide a good beginning for the serious student, who can then find more problems in any ordinary arithmetic book. Also note that problems in multiplication and division may be used as problems in addition and subtraction respectively.

The exercises are arranged so that a student can measure his progress against the yardstick of the Japanese licensing system, the required standard of proficiency for the particular grade being given at the beginning of each group. The possessor of a first, second or third grade license, as awarded by the Abacus Committee, is officially qualified for employment in a public corporation or business house. Licenses for the lower grades are given on the basis of unofficial examinations conducted by numerous private abacus schools.

The exercises are also chosen to give the maximum of variety to the problems, with each digit from zero to nine receiving equal attention—an essential requirement for improvement in abacus operation. The system followed is that just initiated by the Central Abacus Committee after long and careful research.

I. Sixth Grade Operator

Group A

(1 set per minute, or entire group with 70%
accuracy in 10 minutes.)

(1)	(2)	(3)	(4)	(5)
528	967	482	106	815
160	239	251	543	302
427	650	147	928	491
951	108	598	710	852
719	243	120	954	− 169
452	758	− 643	329	− 401
106	491	− 839	267	− 958
843	536	304	695	576
385	702	987	514	740
690	871	439	870	183
724	460	− 671	308	− 235
381	629	− 305	796	− 673
203	984	− 526	632	340
579	315	760	807	927
634	870	215	481	264
7,782	8,823	1,319	8,940	3,054

(6)	(7)	(8)	(9)	(10)
360	769	241	654	185
829	420	952	516	730
213	195	309	740	698
308	− 513	756	495	246
497	− 854	487	536	809
932	508	360	− 785	953
589	274	617	− 320	721
690	421	508	− 197	370
147	963	873	201	617
674	− 307	420	873	164
850	− 631	196	124	902
201	− 175	689	− 482	596
765	286	204	− 968	480
148	840	795	319	342
756	392	138	203	875
7,959	2,588	7,545	1,909	8,688

Group B

(1 set per minute, or entire group with 70%
accuracy in 10 minutes.)

(1)	(2)	(3)	(4)	(5)
728	36	627	52	271
631	87	75	713	6,104
4,089	52	238	60	42
50	705	−94	42	35
92	68	−426	8,096	487
175	96	−81	621	93
47	349	7,513	97	312
904	2,138	59	481	−78
72	510	60	305	−5,083
593	74	−3,041	574	20
61	421	−52	85	961
86	907	139	19	−854
8,260	53	807	73	−69
354	619	40	9,038	−705
13	8,042	968	264	96
16,155	14,157	6,832	20,520	1,632

(6)	(7)	(8)	(9)	(10)
13	806	4,105	936	3,094
624	54	78	21	65
51	−716	29	6,084	413
379	−81	712	−18	817
785	439	67	−745	23
41	5,021	834	−50	71
2,095	48	203	62	938
36	27	40	329	26
984	−78	526	−1,203	7,041
63	−3,605	81	−459	86
542	−953	9,036	48	259
807	130	17	76	95
1,068	69	395	597	508
70	92	58	30	672
92	247	649	817	40
7,650	1,500	16,830	6,525	14,148

Group C

(70% accuracy, 5 minutes.)

(1) $187 \times 53 = 9,911$
(2) $245 \times 21 = 5,145$
(3) $309 \times 19 = 5,871$
(4) $408 \times 38 = 15,504$
(5) $561 \times 60 = 33,660$
(6) $620 \times 42 = 26,040$
(7) $716 \times 90 = 64,440$
(8) $832 \times 57 = 47,424$
(9) $954 \times 74 = 70,596$
(10) $973 \times 86 = 83,678$

Group D

(70% accuracy, 5 minutes.)

(1) $1,725 \times 51 = 87,975$
(2) $2,698 \times 24 = 64,752$
(3) $3,980 \times 30 = 119,400$
(4) $4,509 \times 65 = 293,085$
(5) $5,062 \times 73 = 369,526$
(6) $6,874 \times 68 = 467,432$
(7) $7,431 \times 80 = 594,480$
(8) $8,146 \times 12 = 97,752$
(9) $9,357 \times 49 = 458,493$
(10) $8,230 \times 97 = 798,310$

Group E

(70% accuracy, 5 minutes.)

(1) $960 \div 24 = 40$
(2) $810 \div 45 = 18$
(3) $7,505 \div 79 = 95$
(4) $6,640 \div 80 = 83$
(5) $5,920 \div 16 = 37$
(6) $4,080 \div 68 = 60$
(7) $3,127 \div 53 = 59$
(8) $2,160 \div 30 = 72$
(9) $1,152 \div 72 = 16$
(10) $2,184 \div 91 = 24$

Group F

(70% accuracy, 5 minutes.)

(1) ¥$986 \div 34 = $¥$29$
(2) ¥$855 \div 19 = $¥$45$
(3) ¥$7,280 \div 80 = $¥$91$
(4) ¥$6,240 \div 78 = $¥$80$
(5) ¥$5,092 \div 67 = $¥$76$
(6) ¥$4,128 \div 96 = $¥$43$
(7) ¥$390 \div 13 = $¥$30$
(8) ¥$2,320 \div 40 = $¥$58$
(9) ¥$1,550 \div 25 = $¥$62$
(10) ¥$884 \div 52 = $¥$17$

II. Fifth Grade Operator

Group A

(70% accuracy, 10 minutes.)

(1)	(2)	(3)	(4)	(5)
425	619	502	7,245	167
839	153	698	461	9,035
5,302	762	2,013	956	716
791	8,523	147	179	3,540
514	−478	9,684	317	295
1,283	−694	5,726	420	138
960	−7,081	409	8,096	869
2,048	377	971	−543	327
683	1,049	3,056	−835	5,609
4,067	812	843	2,684	952
794	9,235	329	708	4,786
3,176	−504	760	1,032	128
952	−6,380	4,215	−319	8,073
805	426	837	−908	409
671	905	158	−6,527	241
23,310	7,724	30,348	12,966	35,285

(6)	(7)	(8)	(9)	(10)
895	3,471	912	237	498
7,043	584	463	4,093	6,309
509	628	9,324	308	146
2,918	309	647	7,410	285
451	5,672	1,509	−984	5,037
734	491	854	−2,536	708
1,086	−236	6,082	−841	3,572
427	−7,018	165	965	219
308	4,763	978	8,074	867
872	517	240	129	421
164	902	2,086	715	1,653
6,217	8,059	731	−5,268	820
9,620	−126	3,108	−607	9,046
563	−340	597	259	714
35	−895	375	136	935
31,842	16,781	28,071	12,090	31,230

Group B

(70% accuracy, 10 minutes.)

(1)	(2)	(3)	(4)	(5)
3,128	504	196	837	6,059
940	6,142	2,501	7,590	3,240
8,437	879	385	2,601	918
1,056	−5,263	6,210	9,082	136
9,582	−198	1,479	−649	2,847
365	7,920	8,937	−3,078	9,325
5,297	691	7,068	−429	1,706
7,809	4,702	927	8,563	695
254	9,087	4,253	930	8,014
2,375	6,815	5,406	−358	4,587
718	3,960	8,045	−1,876	273
6,042	−1,536	712	−6,145	7,208
163	−8,473	9,634	7,201	462
4,301	−348	843	5,914	3,159
1,649	2,057	3,521	4,726	5,341
52,116	26,939	60,117	34,909	53,970

(6)	(7)	(8)	(9)	(10)
463	958	7,342	217	592
8,594	149	3,180	1,048	403
3,027	4,807	453	9,731	1,780
−7,380	758	9,508	5,109	6,314
−2,759	3,146	4,261	8,925	509
−902	6,291	937	−2,346	7,921
6,178	530	8,679	−697	2,078
4,813	2,085	518	7,163	8,637
632	5,239	6,024	3,508	981
9,264	7,621	2,187	4,386	3,146
850	1,375	9,840	−6,029	4,065
1,096	8,407	5,706	−275	8,254
−5,709	4,362	695	−5,314	672
−641	9,024	1,039	430	5,890
8,175	613	726	852	9,763
25,701	55,365	61,095	26,708	61,005

Group C

(70% accuracy, 10 minutes.)

(1)	(2)	(3)	(4)	(5)
$ 359	$ 9,535	$ 604	$ 413	$ 2,190
7,569	174	2,895	390	647
408	812	731	706	574
163	3,720	1,048	6,054	1,697
914	−647	269	318	481
792	−1,093	817	8,249	156
5,021	356	4,580	−634	3,078
8,630	2,680	932	−267	423
325	906	126	−9835	310
206	185	658	142	962
127	−263	9,053	5,061	835
4,381	−8,472	316	975	5,289
948	−598	470	−7,529	206
6,057	704	3,749	−807	4,058
874	419	527	182	739
36,774	8,418	26,775	3,418	21,645

(6)	(7)	(8)	(9)	(10)
$ 4,157	$ 516	$ 8,594	$ 740	$ 1,507
823	7,082	250	6,294	960
496	395	913	103	8,023
273	279	−341	857	649
5,082	153	−7,082	5,019	752
761	6,042	361	431	836
−845	821	2,473	520	6,395
−3,978	3,150	749	648	548
−109	264	605	3,976	125
634	4,987	128	837	409
2,014	730	9,086	2,719	287
361	674	−597	301	9,168
−580	968	−1,632	4,658	314
−6,792	401	−805	285	7,431
905	5,893	467	961	270
3,202	32,355	13,169	28,349	37,674

Group D

(70% accuracy, 5 minutes.)

(1) $942 \times 495 = 466,290$
(2) $839 \times 457 = 383,423$
(3) $723 \times 980 = 708,540$
(4) $680 \times 134 = 91,120$
(5) $508 \times 268 = 136,144$
(6) $417 \times 873 = 364,041$
(7) $396 \times 629 = 249,084$
(8) $204 \times 316 = 64,464$
(9) $165 \times 501 = 82,665$
(10) $751 \times 702 = 527,202$

Group E

(70% accuracy, 5 minutes.)

(1) $348 \times 276 = 96,048$
(2) $854 \times 965 = 824,110$
(3) $902 \times 804 = 725,208$
(4) $627 \times 108 = 67,716$
(5) $105 \times 519 = 54,495$
(6) $570 \times 843 = 480,510$
(7) $489 \times 751 = 367,239$
(8) $613 \times 397 = 243,361$
(9) $236 \times 632 = 149,152$
(10) $791 \times 420 = 332,220$

Group F

(70% accuracy, 5 minutes.)

(1) $9,724 \div 26 = 374$
(2) $8,151 \div 13 = 627$
(3) $7,739 \div 71 = 109$
(4) $62,560 \div 80 = 782$
(5) $5,556 \div 12 = 463$
(6) $49,572 \div 54 = 918$
(7) $30,150 \div 67 = 450$
(8) $23,128 \div 98 = 236$
(9) $17,535 \div 35 = 501$
(10) $43,855 \div 49 = 895$

Group G

(70% accuracy, 5 minutes.)

(1) $630,207 \div 90 = 7,023$
(2) $533,484 \div 87 = 6,132$
(3) $420,616 \div 74 = 5,684$
(4) $113,148 \div 63 = 1,796$
(5) $278,772 \div 52 = 5,361$
(6) $85,075 \div 41 = 2,075$
(7) $366,873 \div 39 = 9,407$
(8) $98,504 \div 28 = 3,518$
(9) $72,885 \div 15 = 4,859$
(10) $214,240 \div 26 = 8,240$

III. Fourth Grade Operator

Group A

(70% accuracy, 10 minutes.)

(1)	(2)	(3)	(4)	(5)
6,374	4,561	3,458	9,526	1,459
5,021	9,753	2,983	4,198	3,146
7,913	3,670	4,120	8,973	4,723
9,265	−1,256	6,309	7,269	2,368
4,537	−5,904	5,092	9,085	6,912
5,084	8,329	2,148	−6,450	5,279
8,762	2,048	5,871	−8,317	2,905
7,190	6,827	1,397	−3,802	7,816
3,856	−7,895	7,539	1,236	3,047
4,280	−3,047	2,710	7,084	8,102
8,152	−2,739	6,087	6,735	5,680
2,409	6,180	8,264	−4,391	9,834
6,371	5,912	4,675	−5,140	5,091
1,948	4,106	9,561	2,604	6,470
9,603	1,438	3,406	5,172	7,538
90,765	31,983	73,620	33,782	80,370

(6)	(7)	(8)	(9)	(10)
7,201	2,951	5,482	8,954	6,753
6,759	9,160	8,035	4,710	1,832
1,093	3,294	4,973	3,986	8,094
2,346	8,643	5,106	5,603	2,869
8,712	−4,712	3,683	9,215	7,150
6,507	−1,035	1,290	5,087	3,908
3,874	−5,368	9,624	1,693	9,201
4,158	7,214	2,067	6,854	4,127
8,527	6,870	6,541	2,401	9,382
4,096	5,907	3,712	−6,049	5,240
3,648	−7,582	6,154	−8,731	8,476
5,930	−4,326	7,298	−3,278	6,395
2,489	8,059	4,870	7,142	7,564
1,360	9,781	7,951	9,320	5,013
9,125	6,403	8,309	7,562	4,671
75,825	45,259	85,095	54,469	90,675

Group B

(70% accuracy, 10 minutes.)

(1)	(2)	(3)	(4)	(5)
2,453	5,906	3,629	8,431	9,504
5,192	98,710	41,568	7,846	1,029
67,941	4,825	9,205	20,753	85,934
36,029	5,174	80,453	4,501	2,318
1,683	9,631	−2,687	59,327	−7,840
4,308	3,712	−31,405	7,698	−43,126
8,574	20,893	8,716	3,086	−2,735
3,129	8,074	4,932	64,279	3,052
48,531	2,689	−17,043	1,058	9,607
4,067	60,243	−5,890	6,912	17,269
73,215	87,069	−9,134	2,769	8,573
2,750	1,574	4,716	90,635	−54,618
10,896	6,458	76,352	5,804	−6,481
7,208	53,961	2,879	8,140	70,396
9,645	2,307	5,021	31,972	4,125
285.621	371,226	171,312	323,211	97,007

(6)	(7)	(8)	(9)	(10)
6,712	72,934	1,846	4,165	8,679
3,950	1,653	30,782	1,594	15,032
4,167	3,817	4,935	3,872	6,985
60,843	9,051	8,071	51,943	2,803
5,679	1,329	6,329	92,381	41,697
1,703	−53,682	95,874	−6,705	9,306
29,078	−8,306	3,105	−4,372	5,821
8,634	−2,148	5,763	−87,156	4,068
39,581	80,597	78,491	9,034	37,459
7,824	5,431	40,982	13,507	2,516
2,307	14,970	2,417	5,420	70,128
40,592	−7,026	7,650	7,263	8,749
91,486	−25,469	63,208	−20,489	3,290
6,251	4,205	9,016	−8,016	9,347
8,095	6,748	2,569	2,698	60,175
316,902	104,104	361,038	65,139	286,055

Group C

(70% accuracy, 10 minutes.)

(1)	(2)	(3)	(4)	(5)
$ 2,701	$ 58,976	$ 378	$ 683	$ 8,472
342	4,109	917	50,746	601
60,179	249	4,586	−1,597	7,340
9,630	80,651	1,469	−265	45,981
71,524	1,590	70,354	619	790
8,495	−468	3,042	7,301	13,267
50,723	−5,107	793	25,478	6,154
268	−67,328	2,138	9,032	24,896
956	782	96,205	−359	974
814	3,245	7,621	−40,168	32,058
5,209	92,361	5,839	−8,274	613
43,167	873	19,057	63,921	50,789
1,083	70,934	415	34,580	9,523
548	−3,012	80,246	904	862
86,937	−554	68,120	2,817	1,035
342,576	237,201	361,180	145,418	203,355

(6)	(7)	(8)	(9)	(10)
$ 4,583	$ 75,219	$ 839	$ 13,597	$ 9,218
13,659	327	523	763	40,137
732	139	19,768	27,458	572
403	−6,875	5,017	89,162	1,065
29,581	−906	240	430	56,387
690	50,864	6,754	2,049	941
32,071	8,542	30,482	−98,625	259
947	41,038	1,937	−506	7,308
8,765	−751	684	−4,317	32,596
1,296	−60,218	93,521	5,231	483
95,820	−2,496	8,075	70,318	60,725
7,415	9,547	42,816	−2,679	864
178	37,081	7,109	−985	24,139
80,264	320	24,365	6,140	8,074
6,304	4,693	690	804	1,690
282,708	156,524	242,820	108,840	244,458

Group D
(70% accuracy, 5 minutes.)

(1) $92,854 \times 84 = 7,799,736$
(2) $86,213 \times 59 = 5,086,567$
(3) $73,041 \times 90 = 6,573,690$
(4) $60,378 \times 16 = 966,048$
(5) $51,762 \times 27 = 1,397,574$
(6) $47,609 \times 70 = 3,332,630$
(7) $30,427 \times 32 = 973,664$
(8) $29,185 \times 63 = 1,838,655$
(9) $18,596 \times 45 = 836,820$
(10) $54,930 \times 81 = 4,449,330$

Group E
(70% accuracy, 5 minutes.)

(1) $1,375 \times 562 = 772,750$
(2) $2,610 \times 148 = 386,280$
(3) $3,784 \times 625 = 2,365,000$
(4) $4,208 \times 201 = 845,808$
(5) $5,429 \times 874 = 4,744,946$
(6) $6,057 \times 903 = 5,469,471$
(7) $7,906 \times 417 = 3,296,802$
(8) $8,591 \times 730 = 6,271,430$
(9) $9,832 \times 986 = 9,694,352$
(10) $4,163 \times 359 = 1,494,517$

Group F
(70% accuracy, 5 minutes.)

(1) $9,108 \times 379 = 3,451,932$
(2) $8,240 \times 568 = 4,680,320$
(3) $7,894 \times 740 = 5,841,560$
(4) $6,372 \times 953 = 6,072,516$
(5) $5,423 \times 182 = 986,986$
(6) $4,617 \times 194 = 895,698$
(7) $3,581 \times 807 = 2,889,867$
(8) $2,056 \times 625 = 1,285,000$
(9) $1,905 \times 401 = 763,905$
(10) $3,769 \times 236 = 889,484$

Group G
(70% accuracy, 5 minutes.)

(1) $2,647 \times 3,740 = 9,899,780$
(2) $3,068 \times 2,698 = 8,277,464$
(3) $9,854 \times 7,219 = 71,136,026$
(4) $1,370 \times 4,805 = 6,582,850$
(5) $8,401 \times 6,457 = 54,245,257$
(6) $4,936 \times 9,523 = 47,005,528$
(7) $6,125 \times 5,184 = 31,752,000$
(8) $2,519 \times 8,306 = 20,922,814$
(9) $7,093 \times 1,962 = 13,916,466$
(10) $5,782 \times 3,071 = 17,756,522$

Group H
(70% accuracy, 5 minutes.)

(1)　379,428÷42 = 9,034
(2)　706,860÷85 = 8,316
(3)　235,662÷31 = 7,602
(4)　658,145÷97 = 6,785
(5)　406,164÷68 = 5,973
(6)　　87,362÷19 = 4,598
(7)　115,710÷30 = 3,857
(8)　　55,637÷23 = 2,419
(9)　　94,240÷76 = 1,240
(10)　325,134÷54 = 6,021

Group I
(70% accuracy, 5 minutes)

(1)　　94,235÷401 = 235
(2)　　87,040÷256 = 340
(3)　752,128÷832 = 904
(4)　　64,220÷380 = 169
(5)　548,784÷927 = 592
(6)　431,748÷603 = 716
(7)　385,746÷478 = 807
(8)　219,537÷519 = 423
(9)　107,912÷164 = 658
(10)　620,895÷795 = 781

Group J
(70% accuracy, 5 minutes.)

(1)　636,768÷792 = 804
(2)　　35,984÷208 = 173
(3)　194,394÷537 = 362
(4)　403,425÷815 = 495
(5)　　86,163÷373 = 231
(6)　531,340÷620 = 857
(7)　932,832÷984 = 948
(8)　286,090÷469 = 610
(9)　363,726÷501 = 726
(10)　　74,314÷146 = 509

Group K
(70% accuracy, 5 minutes.)

(1)　553,149÷6,829 = 81
(2)　273,375÷3,645 = 75
(3)　　97,351÷1,453 = 67
(4)　761,664÷7,934 = 96
(5)　　81,018÷4,501 = 18
(6)　　84,942÷2,178 = 39
(7)　424,901÷8,017 = 53
(9)　120,048÷5,002 = 24
(9)　611,640÷6,796 = 90
(10)　394,044÷9,382 = 42

IV. Third Grade Operators

Group A

(70% accuracy, 5 minutes.)

(1)	(2)	(3)	(4)	(5)
$ 8,127	$ 526	$ 105,942	$ 41,306	$ 28,640
659	4,192	835	7,962	135
17,492	60,271	94,516	95,641	86,029
961,037	358,604	62,481	529	401,286
5,208	−963	83,672	890,375	514
638,125	−71,850	1,450	−6,813	37,269
80,734	−5,397	238,107	−380,276	2,478
9,270	409,715	396	784	903,851
25,816	842	740,138	978,250	18,394
401,369	−17,438	253	3,795	549,076
756	−732,609	57,048	12,047	3,702
36,594	90,386	6,729	604,518	153
520,943	6,127	78,915	−421	695,718
481	28,459	406,329	−53,608	4,367
74,308	813,045	9,067	−29,134	70,925
2.780,919	943,910	1,885,878	2,164,955	2,802,537

(6)	(7)	(8)	(9)	(10)
$ 350,624	$ 79,328	$ 60,382	$ 952	$ 14,538
93,041	8,653	847	38,207	751
−68,729	184,705	2,415	706,394	26,374
−134	31,894	531	2,460	652,096
791,560	936	891,270	875	8,725
45,287	507,269	63,092	410,936	479,163
2,759	421	−726	9,283	680
59,641	60,584	−308,619	65,148	13,849
−6,358	245,139	−15,974	931,054	804,975
−804,293	372	704,368	729	5,812
−15,807	4,715	−3,051	54,071	30,427
983	693,807	−57,249	13,567	209
7,410	16,042	425,698	6,182	90,412
362	2,610	9,703	207,648	587,936
201,876	80,597	56,184	89,513	3,160
658,222	1,917,072	1,828,871	2,537,019	2,719,107

Group B

(70% accuracy, 10 minutes. Calculate problems 1–10
to the nearest thousandth; 11–20 to the nearest dollar.)

(1) $4,097 \times 238 = 975,086$
(2) $5,638 \times 149 = 840,062$
(3) $14,902 \times 52 = 774,904$
(4) $7,105 \times 0.098 = 696.29$
(5) $9,674 \times 603 = 5,833,422$
(6) $63.25 \times 7.64 = 483.23$
(7) $853 \times 4.017 = 3,426,501$
(8) $0.3081 \times 0.926 = 0.285$
(9) $2,984 \times 351 = 1,047,384$
(10) $0.2176 \times 87.5 = 19.04$

(11) $\$2,594 \times 376 = \$975,344$
(12) $\$4,608 \times 0.189 = \$871$
(13) $\$7,832 \times 897 = \$7,025,304$
(14) $\$94,120 \times 6.4 = \$602,368$
(15) $\$8,029 \times 738 = \$5,925,402$
(16) $\$975 \times 45.12 = \$43,992$
(17) $\$5,176 \times 0.625 = \$3,235$
(18) $\$3,061 \times 903 = \$2,764,083$
(19) $\$6,843 \times 201 = \$1,375,443$
(20) $\$6,549 \times 643 = \$4,211,007$

Group C

(70% accuracy, 10 minutes. Calculate problems 1–10
to the nearest thousandth; 11–20 to the nearest dollar.)

(1) $937,015 \div 965 = 971$
(2) $0.08988 \div 6.42 = 0.014$
(3) $0.070654 \div 0.136 = 0.520$
(4) $63,366 \div 708 = 89.5$
(5) $55.426 \div 214 = 0.259$
(6) $415,473 \div 591 = 703$
(7) $315.333 \div 45.9 = 6.87$
(8) $280,932 \div 82 = 3,426$
(9) $17.316 \div 0.037 = 468$
(10) $241,893 \div 7,803 = 31$

(11) $\$99 \div 0.368 = \$269$
(12) $\$83,619 \div 27 = \$3,097$
(13) $\$71,967 \div 149 = \$483$
(14) $\$649,612 \div 7,061 = \$92$
(15) $\$560 \div 0.875 = \$640$
(16) $\$415,693 \div 593 = \$701$
(17) $\$33,154 \div 60.5 = \$548$
(18) $\$2,485 \div 2.84 = \$875$
(19) $\$122,536 \div 901 = \$136$
(20) $\$54 \div 0.432 = \$125$